Parables for Now

By the Same Author

More Parables for Now

PARABLES FOR NOW

Edmund Flood

Illustrated by Penelope Burns

Dimension Books · Denville, New Jersey

First USA edition published by Dimension Books, Inc.

First published in Great Britain in 1981
Darton, Longman and Todd Ltd
89 Lillie Road
London SW6 1UD

© 1981 Edmund Flood
Illustrations © 1981 Darton, Longman and Todd Ltd

ISBN 0-87193-186-9

British Library Cataloguing in Publication Data

Flood, Edmund
  Parables for now.
  1. Jesus Christ – Parables
  I. Title
  226'.8'06   BT375.2

Contents

CHAPTER 1	Speaking in Parables	1
CHAPTER 2	What is Jesus offering us?	8
	The Prodigal Son	11
	The Lost Sheep and *the Lost Coin*	21
	The Workers in the Vineyard	32
	The Great Supper	43
	The Two Sons	50
CHAPTER 3	What Happens Now?	57
	The Mustard Seed and *the Leaven*	58
	The Seed Growing Secretly	63
	The Tares and *the Dragnet*	69
	The Sower	75
CHAPTER 4	What did Jesus say about his Teaching in Parables?	80
ENDNOTES		87

Acknowledgement

Except where otherwise indicated, biblical quotations are taken or adapted from the Jerusalem Bible, published and © 1966, 1967 and 1968 by Darton, Longman and Todd Ltd and Doubleday and Co. Inc., and are used by permission of the publishers.

CHAPTER 1 Speaking in Parables

A quick-witted manager, a smart dealer, a drunken butler, a man trudging down the village street at night for help; employees jealous of their differentials, enterprising employees, canny employees, joyful employees; beggars and plutocrats, kings and peasants, fashionable hosts and children. The cavalcade of characters in Jesus' parables is longer yet. Their author clearly relished the humour and variety of human life.

But of course he comes across to us as so much more than a mere observer. He knows how people feel. That sense of cold dismay that that beaten-up man must have felt as first the Priest and then the Levite went on past him, leaving him half dead by the roadside. Or the delight of the woman and her neighbours when she found that coin. Emotions that all of us have felt are experienced by the people in these stories.

So just a glance through Jesus' parables gives us a portrait of the artist as someone fascinated with the whole spectrum of human life. No aloof religious teacher or ticker-tape oracle. He drew his stories from life.

But why did Jesus tell stories? The Gospels make clear that his overriding aim was to announce the chance of a life-time, the supremely good news, that God was coming to live with his people in his *full* power: the 'Kingdom' or rule of God was here. So we might expect dramatic statements. Instead we get estate-managers, dealers, butlers, children and the rest.

One reason why Jesus almost exclusively taught in parables becomes apparent as we read them. We find that they are concerned with human action. They don't tell us about people's fine ideas or beautiful thoughts, or even what they look like, but about what they *do* and about what they feel and think as they do it.

Now this is just what Jesus was interested in. The full

coming of God wasn't just a fine idea or a beautiful thought; it was something you decided to get involved in. It was where a man or a woman chose to enter into a real partnership with God himself in what he wants to do in the world. And an intimate partnership between people, we know, requires a common approach to what they undertake together.

In his parables, therefore, Jesus tried to help people understand what he was doing. They are his self-portrait. They show us what he thought about himself. They offer this so that we can come close enough to him in our approach to life to share with him.

We know how people come close enough to share. Isn't it how we judge the success of a marriage or friendship? We know the effort it takes to understand and appreciate another person's deepest attitudes and feelings. Few of us change these easily. We've probably had them a long time and we may have come to take them for granted in the landscape of our lives. If someone else, even our wife or husband, tells us we're wrong or that *their* views are better, we're likely to go onto the defensive.

This is the other reason why Jesus taught in parables. A parable isn't a blunt instrument that tries to force you to your knees. That would instantly arouse our defensive instincts. No, it's an invitation to escape for a while from everyday life and to step into a world of make-believe. It's like being asked to try on the emperor's clothes. For a time we lose ourselves in a different personality and perhaps a different world and we ask ourselves, intrigued, what it feels like to 'be' the emperor, or the shepherd who lost a sheep, or the widow who couldn't get her rights from the local magistrate.

In a world of make-believe we don't immediately sense that our views or emotions are being questioned. There's a strategically vital gap – perhaps no more than a few seconds, when we feel happy with the shepherd who found that sheep or dismayed at the elder son's refusing his father's invitation to celebrate the younger son's return. Jesus reminds us through his story *what it feels like* to get back something you'd desperately wanted to recover or to see someone standing complacently apart from the warm natural joy of an unexpected home-coming. He gives us the 'feel' of an attitude so that we experience for ourselves how human and right it is and may feel deeply moved by it. And then he asks us to apply the experience he has given us to *our* situation. Is there something in my life that I should feel about in just that way? To have the courage to face up to that is indispensable, he says, if we are to share with him in the Kingdom of God.

An extraordinarily 'modern' approach no doubt. Jesus was putting into practice twenty centuries ago the important 'discoveries' of modern psychologists. They tell us that a blunt kind of teaching converts no one and that you must start from where your audience is. But Jesus, as we know, didn't invent this 'modern' technique called the parable. The Jews had been familiar with it for centuries. Indeed perhaps the best example of how a parable is intended to work is the one that had been told to King David a thousand years before.

Here Nathan obviously had what must have seemed an almost impossible task. He knew that David had fallen in love with this beautiful woman, discovered to his dismay that she was already someone else's wife, and got her husband killed in battle so that he might marry her. If we knew someone who had done that kind of thing we might well find the task of persuading them to be sorry for their deed a formidable one. But Nathan had to do this with an oriental king!

David could visualize what happened in the story Nathan now told him. He knew plenty of rich men with many sheep. And he could picture the poor man with only one sheep who 'grew up with him and his children, eating his bread, drinking from his cup. It was like a daughter to him.' Nathan was telling all this as fact. And when he went on to say that the rich man took the poor man's only sheep and killed it, David exploded with indignation. 'As God lives,' he swore, 'the man who did this deserves to die.'

Like the basically humane person he was, David had naturally taken the part of the poor man. The story had made it possible for him to experience such a wrong *from the standpoint of the person wronged*. So David swore that the wrongdoer must be punished. 'You are the man', was Nathan's reply.

David had the honesty to accept the application. 'I have sinned', he confessed. What the parable had done was to make it psychologically possible for him to apply the goodness that was in him to the wrong he had committed and to see it, for himself, for what it really was.

Jesus does the same in his parables. He holds up a bit of life for us that we can get involved in without a feeling that we're being got at. How does this look to you? he asks us. He addresses us as people who want to be good and honest. He respects our right and vocation to make our own moral decisions. So we look freely to the event it describes. Then comes the crunch: the moment of cowardice or courage. Will I allow myself to see where that attitude is applicable to how *I* am living? Jesus wants me to see the world as it really is, because he wants me to join him in what he is doing there.

Well, what *is* he doing there? What *does* he want to do through us? Since his parables contain most of what he said about that, reflection with all the honesty a parable demands could be the best answer. But Jesus of course didn't drop down from the clouds and utter some parables. He was, like all of us, a person of his time who lived in a certain way and by doing so fulfilled or disappointed the expectations people had of him. He talked about the coming of God, but he acted and spoke as though he was himself very specially related to that coming. In the way he lived and in the relations he formed with people you could, if you opened your eyes, see that. So his parables were largely told to help you understand and appreciate what you had already seen in him.

At a time when so many of his compatriots believed that the long-promised, long-awaited coming of God in his full power was imminent, Jesus took up the proclamation of John the Baptist that that coming was breaking in now. People believed that when the Messiah would come there would be healings and that the Messiah would be known for his compassion. And here before their eyes Jesus was performing healings and was befriending the rejected.

So that was the question about Jesus: could this man from

the provincial uplands really be the herald (and even in some sense the embodiment?) of the Kingdom? Was he the person through whom God would at last bring together his beloved people?

Long ago, with tenderness and affection, he had promised that he would:

> You whom I brought from the confines of the earth
> and called from the ends of the world;
> you to whom I said, 'You are my servant,
> I have chosen you, not rejected you,'
>
> do not be afraid, for I am with you;
> stop being anxious and watchful, for I am your God,
> I am holding you by the right hand;
> I tell you, 'Do not be afraid,
> I will help you.'
> The Holy One of Israel is your liberator.
> (Isaiah 41: 9–14)

This is the half-hearted melody that runs through all the parables. In Jesus' time the spirit of the Jewish people had lost much of its brightness. They had become largely fragmented into exclusive groups, so that their sense of brotherhood and sisterhood was dulled. Their conception of their relationship to their God tended to have more to do with law than with love. But a people whose main source of inspiration was their Scriptures could never entirely forget that at the very centre of human destiny are the infinite possibilities of God's love of his people.

They'd known that for too long for the memory to vanish. More than seven centuries before, the prophet Hosea had realized that God would never abandon them. It was true that they were 'diseased through their disloyalty'. But God *could* not give them up:

> Ephraim, how could I part with you?
> Israel, how could I give you up?
> My heart recoils from it,
> my whole being trembles at the thought.
> I will not give rein to my fierce anger,
> I will not destroy Ephraim again,

for I am God, not man:
I am the Holy One in your midst
and have no wish to destroy.
>   (Hosea 11: 7–9)

In his parables Jesus appeals to that consciousness that was at the heart of his people's experience. Not just as a memory of long ago, but as the clue to what he was offering them now.

Was that memory coming true now, before their eyes? It told of a compassionate God: was this a God-like compassion in their midst? It said that God would lovingly bring together his scattered, fragmented people: was Jesus doing that in the openness of his welcome to all?

So as we explore Jesus' parables, we shan't see them like a general's orders to his troops but as a person speaking to a friend on a matter of great concern. Jesus' contemporaries used parables as 'dark perplexing sayings that were meant to stimulate hard thinking'.[1] So did Jesus. He wanted his friends to think. He wanted them to penetrate so far as they could the profound things he had to offer them.

To help them do that he used every means available. There was their race's long experience of God and of the hope given by his promises that Jesus evoked in many of his parables. There was his listeners' own experience of everyday life and of him. Instead of attacking the bad or the defective in them, he built on the good, gently inviting them to follow that to its true conclusions. He wouldn't push them. He cared too much for their dignity to do that. They must make their own path.

So we shall be seeing in Jesus that touchstone of anyone's character: how he or she communicates with people.

A word, finally, on how this book is arranged.[2] I have started with the parables that are largely concerned with Jesus himself. What did this baffling man think he was doing? In the first five parables I take, Jesus was trying to help people assess the evidence about that.

Then, if you came to recognize Jesus and joined him, what then? The other six parables considered in this book are about some of the implications of following Jesus. Then the last chapter draws out what we've already seen about Jesus' desire to communicate his good news by considering what he said about that and by noticing a widespread misunderstanding.

For each parable I give a reconstruction of the original text so far as possible, then a commentary, and a few reflections that may be of some help to those who wish to reflect on the parables prayerfully. Notes on some more detailed points follow for those who want a fuller kind of exploration. Technical explanations, designed only for the specialist, are buried at the back in the form of endnotes. The superior ([1]) numbers in the text refer to these endnotes.

CHAPTER 2 What is Jesus offering us?

The Prodigal Son
The Lost Sheep *and* the Lost Coin
The Workers in the Vineyard
The Great Supper
The Two Sons

When we have leisurely evening meals with close friends, we may forget about our worries and just enjoy their company, the food and the drink. We celebrate that we are friends and can share in one another's lives. We're not afraid to express the things we most care about.

The most obvious thing about Jesus was that he expressed his friendship in this way with people who seemed to have betrayed their responsibilities to their country and their religion. The tax-collectors he regularly dined with were fellow-Jews who collected taxes extortionately from their own countrymen for the hated occupying power. They were known simply as 'sinners'.

This leisurely kind of evening meal has always been an important feature of life in the East. Work is tough. But when the sun sets it has to stop. People can come together and talk. At a feast they do this round the lamp-light far into the night.

The food, and the way it is served, can be quite sophisticated. The talk at the feast can be sophisticated too. Jews have always been able to combine ritual and imagery with naturalness and enjoyment. Like most people they liked stories, and these can have hidden meanings that you have to search for. They can tease your mind and imagination with what they seem to hint at.

In Jesus' time, at least, the houses weren't closed-up affairs.

WHAT IS JESUS OFFERING US?

You didn't ring the bell; you went in. But you didn't eat with anyone. Eating with a person, and especially feasting with him or her, was to declare deep friendship with that person.

But Jesus kept open house. He wanted to declare real friendship even with the hated tax-collectors. This wasn't just because he was sorry for them. It came from his overwhelming sense that God was present in his life in the fullest way. God, for him, was creating, enabling love. He is someone who from the fulness of his own life makes people be themselves more richly. He breaks down the barriers in our lives.

So Jesus *had* to be among the people hemmed in with barriers. This wasn't to dispense gobbets of teaching like a patronizing preacher. He wanted to be *with* such people, to show them practical human love, and to celebrate their coming to life as they responded to the God-life they found in him. So he took every opportunity to be with them, and the best opportunity of all was where there could be leisurely communication and where feelings of trust and friendship could be built up, and where he loved to share in their joy as they increasingly realized what he was offering them.

So his image quickly became the contemptible one of Jesus the Feaster. It wasn't the parties that provoked the contempt, but the people he had the parties with. Hadn't they betrayed their country at a critical time?

But he *intended* to be Jesus the Feaster. Far from apologizing for the image, he stood by it as essential to the kind of person he was. Unless you understood that, you didn't understand him.

The Scriptures could have helped his critics, since a feast was one of the symbols for the full coming of God that had so long been promised:

God will prepare for all peoples
a banquet of rich food, a banquet of fine wines,
of food rich and juicy, of fine strained wines.
On this mountain he will remove
the mourning veil covering all peoples,
and the shroud enwrapping all nations

he will destroy Death for ever.
God will wipe away
the tears from every cheek;
he will take away his people's shame
everywhere on earth,
for God has said so.
That day, it will be said: See, this is our God
in whom we hoped for salvation;
God is the one in whom we hoped.
We exult and we rejoice
that he has saved us.
(Isaiah 25: 6–9)

Jesus was claiming that in him that full coming of God was present. *This* is the day on which it could be said: 'See, this is our God in whom we hoped for salvation', because 'the mourning veil covering all peoples' was here and now being removed, and death and all barriers to human fulfilment were being destroyed. Of course 'we exult and we rejoice that he has saved us', Jesus was saying. But to be won over by the evidence he was pointing to, you had to be attuned, not primarily to grand religious images, but to the life in real people struggling, with all their handicaps, to live.

So Jesus ate and drank with those who would accept this friendship. That was the best way to communicate with people at depth in a really human and effective way. It was simply something that Jesus *had* to do to express his delight at their good fortune. And it was a symbol that had long been used for God's full presence with his people.

THE PRODIGAL SON   Luke 15: 11–32

'A man had two sons. The younger said to his father, "Father, let me have the share of the estate that would come to me." So the father divided the property between them. A few days later, the younger son got together everything he had and left for a distant country where he squandered his money on a life of debauchery.

When he had spent it all, that country experienced a severe famine, and now he began to feel the pinch, so he hired himself out to one of the local inhabitants who put him on his farm to feed the pigs. And he would willingly have filled his belly with the husks the pigs were eating but no one offered him anything. Then he came to his senses and said, "How many of my father's paid servants have more food than they want, and here am I dying of hunger! I will leave this place and go to my father and say: Father, I have sinned against heaven and against you; I no longer deserve to be called your son; treat me as one of your paid servants." So he left the place and went back to his father.

While he was a long way off, his father saw him and was moved with compassion. He ran to the boy, clasped him in his arms and kissed him tenderly. Then his son said, "Father, I have sinned against heaven and against you. I no longer deserve to be called your son." But the father said to his servants, "Quick! Bring out the best robe and put it on him; put a ring on his finger and sandals on his feet. Bring the calf we have been fattening, and kill it; we are going to have a feast, a celebration, because this son of mine was dead and has come back to life; he was lost and is found." And they began to celebrate.

Now the elder son was out in the fields, and on his way back, as he drew near the house, he could hear music and dancing. Calling one of the servants he asked what it was all about. "Your brother has come," replied the servant, "and your father has killed the calf we had fattened because he has got him back safe and sound." He was angry then and refused to go in, and his father came out and spoke kindly with him: but he answered his father, "Look, all these years I have slaved for you and never once disobeyed your orders, yet you never offered me so much as a kid for me to celebrate with my friends. But, for this son of yours, when he comes back after swallowing up your property – he and his women – you kill the calf we had been fattening."

The father said, "My son, you are with me always and all I have is yours. But it was only right we should celebrate and rejoice, because your brother here was dead and has come to life; he was lost and is found."[1]

The Jews knew God not only to be loving but also to befriend especially the less fortunate and the less respected. God's power could make up for lack of human clout. Its scope wasn't confined by human yardsticks.

One way in which this was conveyed was by God's frequent choice of the *younger* brother. As soon as Jesus' audience heard of a younger brother in this story, they would have recognized a theme song that ran throughout the Bible.[2]

Jacob, they knew, had been chosen instead of the elder Esau, Joseph instead of his elder brothers, David instead of his. But it was a woman who had most clearly typified God's special love for the less respected. In the story of Judith, 'a mere woman' – as she would then have seemed – defeated a powerful invader at a time of national crisis. The Assyrians were 'boasting in their army, glorying in their horses and their riders, exulting in the strength of their infantry.' Judith expressed to God her confidence that he could use 'a mere woman' to overcome them:

> Since you are the God of the humble,
> the help of the oppressed,
> the support of the weak,
> the refuge of the forsaken,
> the saviour of the despairing.
> (Judith 9: 11)

The story of Judith is an allegory to celebrate God's way of bringing life. He can support even the weak. No disaster and no lack of human respect can put a person who trusts in him beyond his power to bring to life. As Judith sees so clearly when she has defeated the Assyrians, God's work among his people is like an ever-continuing creation:

> You spoke and things came to be,
> you sent your breath and they were put together,
> and no one can resist your voice.
> Should mountains topple
> to mingle with the waves,
> should rocks melt
> like wax before your face,
> to those who fear you,
> you would still be merciful.
> (Judith 16: 14–15)

But who were the weak, the forsaken and the despairing who were being brought to new life by God's continuing creation that Jesus was referring to in his story? Some of the people round that very table. People who had done terrible things, but who had, against all human probability, turned back to God.

Jesus was using what his listeners already knew about feasting and God's favouring the less esteemed like younger sons and women. In this story he was trying to help them to use that knowledge to understand that his own feasting and his own association with the weak and the forsaken might be quite different from the scandalous thing many of them felt it to be. The story might help them to see his actions in a totally different light.

So his story started with two sons, with the focus on the younger. This son wanted to emigrate, so he asked his father, a farmer, for a share of the property.[3]

In Middle Eastern thinking, it was an outrageous request. A son making it would have been thought to want his father's death.

That would not have been the case, of course, if *the father* had made the suggestion. In fact, fathers would quite often divide up the estate between their sons, so as to avoid disputes after their own death. But in those cases, the estate wasn't broken up, since no land was sold. This case was quite different. Not merely was the younger son making what was thought of as an utterly heartless request of his father, to transfer rights in the estate that made the father count for him as good as dead, but also he was asking for part of the estate *to be sold*: he wanted it in money, now.

At this point in Jesus' story his audience would have expected the father to explode with anger and beat the boy for this extraordinarily impertinent request. Instead they hear that the request was granted. The son was given his eventual share, and a right to sell it immediately. The family estate is a significant part of the Middle Easterner's personal identity. It would be zealously preserved and handed on within the family. Even if the father was incredibly allowing all this, the local community would have been shocked and angry. So the son left as soon as possible, before the local situation got too hot for him.

The son went abroad and squandered the money in reckless living. And then there came one of the famines to which the Middle East was prone. He had arrived as a man of means, but was now forced to be a 'hanger-on' of some wealthy man. Probably in order to get rid of him, the rich man offers him a job that a Jew would normally not dream of accepting. Pig-keeping, for the Jews, was a bye-word for human degradation. To the amazement of Jesus' audience, the boy accepts the job. But even here he wasn't getting enough to keep himself alive, and in his destitution the boy realizes how much better off he would be in his father's home. He would ask his father to make him a hired servant.

His wages would eventually give back to his father the protection of which he had robbed him.

Jesus told the story in such a way as to call to his audience's minds a similar change of heart in the Scriptures they knew so well. They too painted a vivid and moving picture of how terrible deprivation had brought such a change. 'I will go back to my first husband, I was happier then than I am today', the wife had said in her misery. So this wife (who stood for Israel), went back to God, her loving husband. God longed for his homecoming. He said to his erring wife:

> I will betroth you to myself for ever,
> betroth you with integrity and justice,
> with tenderness and love.
> (Hosea 2: 19)

Jesus' audience was clearly meant to see this younger son's homecoming as reminiscent of Israel's homecoming to God in Hosea. This isn't to say that the father represents God (and the younger son, Israel). Jesus is simply saying to the listeners to the story: you recognize this kind of relationship as typical of God's with his people: God longing for his beloved people to come back to him: the people taught by hardship to repent; the eager, delighted welcome and embrace.[4]

And what a welcome it turned out to be! Jesus' audience could easily picture the hornet's nest the younger son was about to enter. The entire village community would have had it in for him: this young man who had let down his father, broken up a local estate, and not content even with that, had handed over the proceeds to foreigners. The family house would have been in the village (landowners' houses weren't usually on open land). As the younger son approached the village, news would quickly have spread and deep feelings of disgust would be made clear by groups, who could easily coalesce to form an angry mob. In the full public gaze of the hostile and perhaps jeering crowd there came this prominent and elderly man of the village doing what respectable citizens never did: he was running! And he was running towards this disgraced intruder. The stately walk expected of him was too slow for his impatience to show his love and forgiveness. Hence that undignified, eager rush, the warm embrace, the eagerness to do the son restored to him every possible kind of honour (see Note III) and to celebrate this marvellous good fortune, as he saw it, with the whole household. Again there is a strong suggestion that this is typical of God's way of loving. The description was reminiscent of how Esau had received and forgiven the brother who had wronged him. Esau, too, had run to Jacob, taken him in his arms and embraced him. And Jacob had recognized in that the goodness of God.[5]

As the younger son had approached the village, his heart must have been in his boots at the jeers and the taunts he would be likely to meet with from the villagers. But he knew his father was an exceptionally generous man – what other father would have given in to his earlier request? His plan was to endure the initial unpleasantness, and by earning wages and not living in the family home to win back by his own efforts freedom from indebtedness to his father and his own self-respect, without sponging off his father or elder brother.

But he never makes the request he has been rehearsing. The father has a different plan for him. He's not interested in the boy *earning back* his favour but in his *accepting* it.

And that was much more difficult, of course, than it sounds. It was easy to imagine how the elder brother would react to a full reinstatement of his renegade brother. And *earning* one's self-respect is much more attractive than being given it.

But he overcame these difficulties, abandoned his plan for eventual self-satisfied independence, and threw himself completely into his father's spirit of gracious kindness and celebration. He would let him *be* a father to him, and now he would be a son. Were those listening to the story meant to ask themselves whether the same readiness to abandon smug independence and accept generous love was just as admirable in Jesus' friends – their despised brother-Jews?

With the arrival of the younger son, everyone present is drawn into that re-establishment of true relationship. The servants are told to dress him with the father's special robe for great occasions, so that everyone can see that the disgraced man now shares the father's favour and status; and it isn't just a question of silencing the villagers' hostility or of showing them the man's new status: the killing of a fatted calf means a feast for the whole village. It provides enough food for over a hundred people and has to be eaten within a few hours. The father is treating the occasion as a farmer would the marriage of his elder son, or the visit of the governor of a province: the village community must be invited to the celebration.

The elder son in Jesus' story is out in the fields, and he hears the music and dancing as the party starts to get under way. He asks one of the young boys outside the house what it's all for. He is told that it is for the recovery of his brother. As elder brother he would be expected to welcome back and congratulate his brother and to play a major part in looking after the guests. But he can't see that his brother's return demands celebration; he is angry and won't go in. The public refusal to come in would have seemed to the villagers extremely insulting: a queen had been deposed by her husband for such a refusal. But the father's response to this insult is once again that day to leave his house to offer affectionate reconciliation. He speaks kindly with him[6] and asks him to join the celebrations; but even this doesn't appease his son's anger. The son brusquely replies that his younger brother has done great wrong, while he has always striven to do right. Favours like a kid – let alone a fatted calf – should be given only to those who have worked for them. The language of the pay-deal, not that of forgiveness and joy, is the only one he chooses to understand. A party to celebrate his brother's homecoming is offensive.

To see the full force of the elder brother's refusal, we have to consider the movement of the story. It starts with a man 'having' two sons. The first half of the story involves us movingly in a sequence of events which threatens to break permanently his 'having' one of those sons. It is told in such a way that the audience is being helped to experience the goodness of the eventual restoration of the younger son to the father. But it isn't yet a restoration of the father 'having *two* sons'. The wholeness of the family is not yet restored.

The second half of the story is told so as to involve us in

the question as to whether that wholeness will in fact be restored. The elder son has remained at home with the father. But now that the younger son is being welcomed back, the father's situation has changed. The elder son will accept the father's new situation only if he joins in the party. If he does, the threat to the father's 'having' two sons will be over and the wholeness required by the story will have been achieved.

This second half of the story maintains tension throughout as to whether the elder son will accept this situation or not. He 'draws near' the party – but doesn't yet go in. On hearing the explanation for the party he angrily refuses to go in – but his father comes out to 'speak kindly with him'. The elder son's response is to reject still more radically the family's restoration to its original wholeness. He won't call the returned man his 'brother' – he's just a traitor-son. He implies that he himself has hardly been treated as a son.

The father makes one more attempt to restore the family's wholeness. He begins by calling the man affectionately 'my son', and then reminds him how close they have always been. They've shared their lives; the property actually belongs to the elder son; and isn't the man whose return is being celebrated his brother?

Jesus doesn't tell us the elder brother's reply to that last gentle but eager pleading. The ending wasn't given by the story-teller: it was left for the listener to fill in.[7] He was the elder brother who could respond to that offer of love, that invitation to the mutual acceptance, the wholeness that is man's real destiny, and especially the destiny of God's chosen people. Or he could refuse.

REFLECTION

1. Has there ever been such a picture of God? Not of a God 'out there', but God as experienced by people at the very heart of our emotions and attitudes. This is the God that Jesus knew was in him, eagerly and tenderly offering his love to the men and women around him. This, Jesus is saying, is the coming of God's Kingdom, which fills my whole being and which I want you to have.

2. Our first reaction to this parable is likely to be delight that such things are. All the details of the story enhance that delight. Each of us will make our own choice. That close observation of village life; the irrepressible, tender kindness of the father; the clear message that a real relationship with God depends on our accepting ourselves as having done wrong and himself as eager to forgive, to love, and to rejoice with us that now we are together and that all he has is ours.

3. The elder brother in the story is there to remind us that we can get that relationship tragically wrong – just as we know we can get marriage or friendship wrong by not really accepting that we are lovable for the other, or not really loving them. Is it true to say that the elder brother loves not people but principles? He wants to be a rock, an island if necessary, of moral achievement. He represented all that Jesus, this 'revolutionary' religious teacher, was most opposed to and all that was most frustrating his teaching of success. But the elder brother is *not* the villain of the story. The whole story is a delicate and poignant invitation to him to come in.

4. 'The world is a unity, and we must begin to act as members of it who depend on each other. . . . We have to lift ourselves above the immediate constrictions, and offer the world a plan and a vision of hope, without which nothing substantial can be achieved.' (*North-South: a programme for survival*, Willy Brandt and others, 1980, p. 47★)

NOTES

I. The story suggests that when the younger son received his share, the father made over the rest of the inheritance to the elder (while retaining the actual use of it throughout his own life – a common practice then). But in that case he would have had no

★This Report was the result of an independent investigation by a group of international statesmen and leaders from many spheres, headed by the former Chancellor of Germany. The eighteen members of the commission came from five continents and different points of the political spectrum.

right to reinstate the younger son with authority over the property. There seems to be an inconsistency here, and 'the question of any further inheritance by the younger son is simply not raised in the dramatic setting of the parable.'[8]

II. It seems that we are meant to understand the younger son as truly repentant, even though 'to come to his senses' probably expressed repentance in a qualified sense. The allusions to Hosea 2: 19 and to Jeremiah 31: 18–20 seem to make this sincerity clear.[9]

III. The ring, given to the younger son by command of the father, was a symbol of authority, and the shoes were the symbols of authority, possession and freedom.[10]

THE LOST SHEEP Matthew 18:12–14, and Luke 15:4–7

'What man of you having a hundred sheep and losing one of them does not leave the ninety-nine in that desolate hill country and go after the lost sheep until he finds it? And when he has found it he places it upon his shoulders rejoicing. Then, when he arrives back home, he calls to his friends and neighbours: "Rejoice with me, because I have found my sheep which was lost." I say to you that there is more joy with God over one sinner who was lost, than over ninety-nine righteous persons who were not.'

We are responsible for something important in our job, and suddenly we lose control. If we can't regain control, we ourselves and our family will suffer. Then suddenly, when catastrophe seems imminent, we manage to pull out of that plunge to disaster. What happiness! Might there not even be a celebration?

It is just like that with this shepherd. In rough, remote country he's tending the sheep that belong to several families of his village, including perhaps sheep of his own. Thieves, wild animals and the rough terrain make his task difficult.

Any loss would damage not only his own reputation as a shepherd and make it difficult for him to find re-employment; it would also be damaging to the village he comes from. Agricultural communities had evolved their own insurance system, and this meant that anyone who came across the strayed sheep would in most cases not be entitled to ignore it but would be obliged to spend time and perhaps money in trying to find the owner.[1]

This shepherd does in fact, probably through his own negligence,[2] lose the sheep. He leaves the rest of the flock with his mates and goes in search of the lost sheep. He is determined to search for it 'until he finds it'.

To his joy he does find it. But a lost sheep will lie down helplessly and refuse to budge.[3] So now he has to carry it on his shoulders.[4] The rest of the flock would be driven back to the village that evening as they were every evening, so he carries the lost sheep back there.[5] Obviously this would have needed great endurance; and yet to our surprise he *rejoices* at it!

Eventually he reaches the village, and now he asks his friends and neighbours to join him in celebrating this good fortune, that in various ways involves them all.

It's not so much the success of his seeking that is the subject of his celebration, or the value of the individual sheep, but the fact that *once again the flock is intact*. For him, that means he isn't the kind of shepherd that loses sheep; and for his neighbours it means he isn't a financial liability.

The story-teller makes it clear that the point of the parable is the recovery of the flock's wholeness by making the parable turn, in both its key moments, on a paradox. At the moment when he loses the sheep and decides to go in search of it, and at the moment when he is celebrating finding it, it is *the recovery of that one sheep* that counts more for that shepherd than anything else.

That the story is about the restoration of a flock's wholeness is made clearer by the use of numbers.[6] The significance of 99 is brought home to us every time we enter a supermarket. Prices like that are put on goods to suggest to us that we're not quite spending $100 or £100. '99' is meant to reassure us (whether successfully or not!) that it's 'not the full 100'. When it's a question of our paying money to wealthy supermarket chains, we may be glad of the incompleteness! But in the context of his flock, that *completeness* was just what the shepherd wanted. Jesus goes out of his way to underline this by giving us the otherwise odd information that the flock left behind consisted of just ninety-nine sheep.

What was Jesus getting at? Why was he telling them this story? Obviously to help them understand what he was doing. Most inexplicable and even scandalous about that was his habit of dining with those extortioners, those traitors to their country, the tax-collectors, and also with other people

THE LOST SHEEP

with jobs that involved them in breaking the Law: people who also were contemptuously called 'sinners'.

Jesus seemed to be suggesting that in his welcome to these people there was a finding that just *had* to be celebrated. No doubt his listeners could see the joy he experienced in welcoming these despised people. In this story he seemed to ask them to share in the joy. And what could have made that especially clear to them was this delight of the shepherd not only in finding that lost sheep but in restoring the wholeness of the flock.

Jesus' audience knew that God had promised long ago a similar restoration to *his* flock:

> I am going to look after my flock myself.
> I shall rescue them from wherever they have been
> scattered during the mist and the darkness. . . .
> I shall look for the lost one, bring back the stray,
> bandage the wounded and make the weak strong.
> (Ezekiel 34:11–16)

But in Jesus' time, as we have seen, this great vision was far from being fulfilled. The Jews were a people torn by mutual scorn and division.

You saw the Pharisees, for example, holding that *they* were the genuine members of God's people, the 'true Israel', and despising the ordinary people as unfaithful to God's law. Or those groups of monks at Qumran, near Jericho, who saw themselves as God's true people, surrounded by the 'Sons of Darkness'.

You had the Zealots and the Sicarii, who saw force as the only answer to Israel's problems. And distanced from all these groups, and despised by them all, were the general mass of the people.

So Israel in Jesus' time was a fragmented people, a sick nation. Each of those groups had started in quest of that vision of a united people, the one people of God. But each had eventually succumbed to fanaticism.

And here, quite suddenly, was someone who wanted to bring the fragments together, as John the Baptist had tried to do. His welcome was for *everyone*. The Pharisee-type to whom the story of the Prodigal Son offered that open door;

the Zealots, who were so numerous in the Galilean towns and villages, and who must have been among his friends; but above all the ordinary people, and the more cut-off they were the greater the trouble he took with them: the sick, the lepers, and the despised 'law-breakers'.

Because he sympathized with them and loved them? Yes: you had only to see that old man running down the village street to embrace his son to realize that. But even more than that because he wanted there to *be* a people of God again: there had to be a tangible, convincing sign to all mankind that there is a real God at the heart of every man and woman's life, and it isn't teaching or books that can persuade people of that, but a lived and shared experience of such a God.

With all his mind and heart he wanted that. 'Jerusalem, Jerusalem, how often have I longed to gather your children, as a hen gathers her brood under her wings' (Luke 13:34). Not by stinging rebuke, but by what he hoped people would come to see as the evident rightness of his welcome to all, and by the gentle nudging of his stories, he wanted them *all* to rise above their entrenched prejudices and come into the Kingdom together.

He wanted them to receive what from the depths of his experience he knew he had to give: a dream come true, a vision realized. No one really knows how those who had first dreamed it, centuries before, thought it would come true. But for so long now it had haunted the imagination and given hope for the future. Jesus' listeners knew those old prophecies about Israel, God's 'servant':

> Here is my servant . . .
> my chosen one in whom my soul delights.
> I have endowed him with my spirit
> that he may bring true justice to the nations . . .
> Faithfully he brings true justice;
> he will neither waver, nor be crushed.
>
> Thus says God,
> he who created the heavens and spread them out,
> who gave shape to the earth and what comes from it,
> who gave breath to its people
> and life to the creatures that move in it.

I, God, have called you to serve the cause of right,
I have taken you by the hand and formed you;
I have appointed you as covenant of the people and light of the nations,
to open the eyes of the blind,
to free captives from prison,
and those who live in darkness from the dungeon.
                    (Isaiah 42: 1–7)

This was the promise: in the midst of the self-interest and cruelty that divides and destroys, a people like that.

Could Jesus be the shepherd who had now come to gather a people together that would really be a 'light to the nations'? His listeners could see his joy as 'he rescued the scattered from the mist and darkness'. And they knew how natural it was for the friends and neighbours of the shepherd to share in celebrating a rescue that affected them all. Could he really be suggesting that they should stop being shocked at his parties and, instead, like the shepherd's fellow-villagers, join in the celebrations themselves?

REFLECTION

1. Like all Jesus' parables, this was an invitation to his listeners to see what was happening before them with fresh eyes. Would his listeners join in the work of making them whole again, a people through whom God could bring light to the world?

The invitation was, as we know, declined. The sick nation would not be gathered together. The person who had drawn attention to its sickness could not be tolerated, and so like Simon in Golding's novel *Lord of the Flies*, he had to be killed. That brief dream seemed over.

Their experience of Jesus living after his death – living a kind of human life that they had no categories to describe, convinced his totally beaten followers that that dream had in fact come true. It was coming true through them. It took time, naturally, for them to work out how the Jewish religion fitted into this. But their central conviction about themselves was that they *must*, after such an experience, be the real Israel, God's people united at last.

Luke so often speaks of this conviction. In the first solemn announcement of his Gospel, we hear that John the Baptist's task will be that of 'preparing a people fit for God' (Luke 1:17). In Mary's song of wonder and thanks about her task, she feels that in her God is 'coming to the help of Israel' (Luke 1:54), to fulfil the promise he had made. The announcement to the shepherds is of 'news of great joy, a joy to be shared *by the whole people*' (Luke 2:10).

So Luke didn't write his two-volume work of his Gospel and the Acts of the Apostles to describe a sad might-have-been of history but to help his contemporaries understand the *significance for them* of the fact that Jesus 'had shown himself alive to the apostles after his passion, by many demonstrations, and had continued to appear to them for forty days and tell them about the kingdom of God' (Acts 1:3). What the Jews rejected, he is saying, is coming true through us. That, he tells us, is the purpose of all followers of Jesus: to be God's people, for all men and women.

2. Through this parable Jesus is asking us, as appealingly and urgently as when he told it to his Jewish listeners, how well we are fulfilling the purpose God has for us.

Could we say that Christians have seldom had greater opportunities of responding to that call?

Until recently we were fragmented by misunderstanding and distrust. In the last two decades great progress has been made in dismantling barriers. Many Christians from all churches realize that far more unites us than divides us.

But we know that just realizing this is not enough. Does the world see us coming together: especially where it chiefly meets us, in our neighbourhood? What are we doing to bring this about? What more should we do? If our leaders sometimes appear to be impeding progress, haven't we a right and even a duty to make our voice heard?

3. This parable is a story of care, sadness, effort and joy. We watch the developing experience of this shepherd and see in that Jesus' own experience among the people he cared for.

THE LOST SHEEP

The story, with its powerful echoes of God's promises that he would one day gather his people, conveys Jesus' consciousness that God's climactic presence and work among his people was happening fully through him.

Shepherding to bring God to people, especially the weak and rejected, was the life he lived and the life he had to offer others. *Only this brought real joy.*

Who needs help where I am? Is God's people in my area one that makes it possible for all to see for themselves the care, effort and joy of the Christ we believe lives in us? Prudence is no doubt necessary in all human affairs. Jesus' own example might suggest to us that courage and boldness are equally indispensable.

NOTES

1. A glance at Matthew and Luke shows that they are stressing different things. For Matthew the important thing is that the shepherd *searches for the sheep*, while for Luke it is *the joy of finding it*. Both points, as we have seen, are marvellous aspects of the good news that Jesus was proclaiming. But neither individually nor together do they do justice to what he was saying.

We know that Matthew in this part of his Gospel wanted to bring out Jesus' concern for the 'little ones': people who are disadvantaged in any way. In this parable he found a perfect illustration of this. He wasn't interested in telling us here the full significance of Jesus' parable, even if it was still remembered. He had a different purpose.

Luke, on the other hand, is trying in this part of his Gospel to show the importance of repentance. True, even the most tractable of sheep could hardly be said to 'repent'! But Jesus' parable did paint quite vividly the joy at the recovery of the lost sheep.

But in the light of the text itself and of what we know about Jesus' life, it seems clear that in this parable Jesus was doing more than what Matthew and Luke show us. He was claiming that in his quest for those who had strayed from the flock his people should recognize the culminating presence of God: the coming of the Kingdom. He wasn't just giving a reminder of long-standing truths, however important; he was trying to help his listeners understand that at this moment they stood at the turning point of history.

It has only recently been recognized that the parable doesn't see the straying sheep merely as one of a flock, but as one whose loss would destroy the flock's wholeness. Jesus was trying to meet the audience's objection that he gave so much of his attention to the 'lost'. Such a disproportion is natural, he is suggesting, both when you lose something you care so much about, and also when you find it. But he is suggesting even more strongly that there is something here of immense significance and joy for his objectors. Can my parable not help you to see, he is asking, that in my care for the lost you are in the presence of the event you have longed for: God's gathering of his people?

II. Does the story imply that the shepherd's decision to go in search for the one sheep endangers the rest? Probably not. As an authority on Palestinian life writes: 'Experts on Palestinian life all agree that a shepherd cannot possibly leave his flock to itself. If he has to look for a lost animal he leaves the others in the charge of shepherds who share the flock with him . . . or drives them into a cave.'[7]

III. It is generally accepted that the parable of the Lost Sheep was spoken by Jesus, because it was so aptly contrived for what he wanted to say. Particularly because of the differences between the versions in Matthew and Luke, there is argument about which parts of the two texts were original. The text given here has been formed in the light of this discussion.[8]

THE LOST COIN Luke 15: 8–9

'What woman who has ten drachmas and who loses one of them does not light a lamp and sweep the house and seek diligently until she finds it? And, when she does find it, does she not call together her friends and neighbours saying, "Rejoice with me, for I have found the coin which I had lost."?'[1]

In this age of banknotes, we may be tempted to assume that the loss of a coin about the size of a dime wasn't worth the fuss given it in this story.[2] But in fact it would have brought you enough to feed quite a large family for a day. So the picture Jesus paints here is not far-fetched. It shows a woman with more than a week's wages, perhaps kept for a special occasion like a family trip to some festival, and somehow she's managed to mislay a tenth of it. It's naturally a serious loss to her. And the scarcity of cash in the largely self-supporting Palestinian villages would have made the loss still heavier.

The *zuz*, as the Jews called this coin, is an ungainly object, since it's neither round nor symmetrical. This had the convenient consequence that it wouldn't roll along the stone floor of the peasant's small house, but just flop and stay put until found. But in windowless houses like these, it wouldn't be easy to find such a small object. So the housewife lights a lamp, and with the help of its light starts sweeping the floor with a palm-twig, hoping it will soon make the coin tinkle on the stone floor.

As she does so she realizes that she and her family aren't the only people with a stake in her attempt to find the coin. Houses like hers weren't closed-up affairs. Her neighbours would have been constantly in and out of her house and would be apt to know where she kept her possessions. Until the coin was found, every woman who had come into the house since its owner had last seen it would fall under suspicion.

Jesus' listeners may, at this point, have been half expecting an unhappy outcome, for the word used to describe several of these coins was *zuzim*, and that also meant 'those that have moved away or departed'. In fact the proneness of these small but valuable coints to 'depart' from their owner had inspired Palestinian wits to compose a riddle: 'Why are coins called *zuzim*?' it asked. 'Because they are removed from one person and given to another!' It looks as though Jesus was alluding to that old riddle, underlining the possibility that lost *zuzim* could well be lost permanently.[3]

All the greater is the joy when the coin is found. Friends and neighbours are 'cleared', and the woman has her money. No wonder she immediately arranges a celebration.

Once again, as in the Lost Sheep parable, a broken wholeness is restored. Perhaps again Jesus is suggesting that his work is to restore Israel to being once more a true people of God.

Such a restoration may be less stressed in this parable. We have to remember that folk-tales like to deal in round numbers; that here it isn't reinforced, as it is in the Shepherd parable, with the image of the flock; and that these two parables may well have been originally separate.[4]

But the woman 'sweeping the house' was probably intended to remind Jesus' listeners of that other 'house', the 'house of Israel'. Shouldn't his listeners, as members of that house, be sharing in his joy at recovering those who had been lost to it? Wasn't his friendship with sinners a matter not for grumbling, but for rejoicing, for the whole of God's people?

REFLECTION

Doctors and nurses know the joy of making people whole again. Many of us, in different ways, have had similar experiences. In such a simple and natural way, Jesus could remind his listeners what it feels like to recover something you value so as to help them look again at what they saw in him. Has our talk about Jesus sometimes obscured from us the character of the person who could illuminate what he was trying to do by telling *this* kind of story?

THE WORKERS IN THE VINEYARD
Matthew 20: 1–15

'The Kingdom of God is like a landowner going out at daybreak to hire workers for his vineyard. He made an agreement with the workers for one denarius a day, and sent them to his vineyard. Going out at about nine he saw others standing idle in the market place and said to them, "You go to my vineyard too and I will give you a fair wage." So they went. At about twelve o'clock and again at about three, he went out and did the same.

Then at about five he went out and found more men standing round, and he said to them, "Why have you been standing here idle all day?" "Because no one has hired us," they answered. He said to them, "You go into my vineyard too."

In the evening, the owner of the vineyard said to his bailiff, "Call the workers and pay them their wages, starting with the last arrivals and ending with the first." So those who were hired at about five came forward and received one denarius each. When the first came, they expected to get more, but they too received one denarius each. They took it, but grumbled at the landowner. "The men who came last", they said, "have done only one hour, and you have treated them the same as us, though we have done a heavy day's work in all the heat." He answered one of them and said, "My friend, I am not being unjust with you; did we not agree on one denarius? Take your earnings and go. I choose to pay the last-comer as much as I pay you. Have I no right to do what I like on my own estate? Why are your hearts filled with rancour because I am good?" '[1]

THE WORKERS IN THE VINEYARD 33

In a well-told story about industrial relationships we feel ourselves involved in a variety of shifting and often conflicting interests and emotions. We may well have experienced a similar situation: perhaps as an employer, who has to keep the business profitable and the work-force happy, as well as caring for their welfare; or as employees, who need to keep our jobs in an unstable world and get a decent wage, and are apt to react strongly against unjust treatment as an affront to our dignity and as dangerous for our economic future.

It was natural for Jesus to take a vineyard as the setting for a story about industrial relationships. Palestine had, of course, long been a country of vineyards. In much of it, vinegrowing was the chief industry.[2] His listeners could follow the story as one does any game of skill. As in industrial relationships everywhere, there was a complex set of options and strategies. The interplay between employer and work-force could be as intricate as any kind of game.[3]

But of course it wasn't just a game. Work, especially then, was necessary for survival. In Palestine the unemployed could starve and watch their families starve. In this complex interplay the stakes could be high.

So Jesus seems to be giving us a story of everyday life based on a Palestinian vineyard. But right from the first sentence his listeners could have begun to suspect that something still more important was being hinted at. Yes, they could recognize the kind of bargains struck, the gambits of the game. They were familiar stuff. Perhaps it *was* just a story. But Jesus had a certain reputation. He was said to be hinting at something momentous or subversive about the Kingdom. For Jesus to take a vineyard, and agreements about working it, as the subject of a story was like a revolutionary publicly telling a story about a fight for national independence.[4]

Today many English-speaking countries have vineyards of good quality. Either at first hand or on television we may have seen the rich, lush colours of the grapes, and the abundance and strength of the plants. Perhaps inevitably they remind us of wine, celebration, and happiness with friends.

The Jews had long known such feelings. But unlike most of us today they didn't think of vineyards as things *other people* tended. They were well aware, often from first hand experience, of the tough, patient work needed.

For centuries they had felt themselves to be *God's* vineyard, where the grapes should be red and of fine quality, and which God loved and cared for and longed to see come to harvest. The harvest would depend, as in any vineyard, on the landowner hiring workers and on their industry and skill.

For Jesus' audience, such agreements were the great landmarks of history which gave human life its meaning. The first agreement (or 'covenant', as they called it) had been with Noah. It was made between God and 'every living thing that is found on the earth' (Genesis 9:12). It promised that there *would be* harvest. The terrible alternative of chaos would not win. Instead this world, teeming with life, under the wise command of men and women would 'be fruitful, multiply and fill the earth'; and people would be God's fellow-workers in his bringing us to our fulfilment.

There had been the covenant with Abraham, where God had promised that Abraham would be 'the father of many nations', and that he would give Abraham's descendants 'this land' (Genesis 17: 2; 15:18). Then the culminating covenant

THE WORKERS IN THE VINEYARD

with Moses, where God had promised this loose collection of people that if they kept their covenant with him they would be his very own people (Exodus 19:5). And another covenant, to develop this still further, with David, promising the king that 'your house and your sovereignty will always stand secure before you, and your throne shall be established for ever.' (2 Samuel 7:16).[5]

So, as Jesus unfolded his story, the more perceptive would have seen this as a teasing, evocative interplay between the down-to-earth laws of a well-known kind of labour-market and a picture of our destiny as God constantly renewed the loving relationship between himself and his people. To be with Jesus was to experience an invitation to achieve a deeper kind of humanity: to move towards an appreciation of attitudes and values. It wasn't strange that in his stories too one could experience a similar kind of invitation. They respect and value everyday life. They do this particularly by inviting us to see our lives in the context that gives them their true purpose.

The story begins. Except for the fact that Jesus is talking about a vineyard, the story begins in a low key. Here is an ordinary farmer anxious to get his crop in, urgently, at the lowest possible cost. So he goes out before dawn to hire workers, since they'll be cheaper then and he wants the full twelve hours work from them. He haggles with them, as orientals love to do, and manages to hire them for a modest wage of one denarius.[6]

The next bit of the story may seem to us far-fetched. Surely only a hopelessly inefficient employer would find as many as four times in one day that he still has insufficient labour? But on the one hand he would be anxious not to hire more workers than necessary, and on the other the harvesting could be urgent. The grapes had to be gathered, packed and pressed at exactly the right time, so that they would have the right sugar-content. And if the critical day was a Friday, failure to finish the harvesting on that day could lead to great loss, since no more work could be done, of course, until Sunday.[7]

Jesus' audience might well have deduced from this constant new hiring that it was indeed a Friday, and the harvest a particularly good one. But the story isn't directly concerned with the harvest but with the agreements with the workforce.

The first agreement, we saw, is through negotiation, probably prolonged, shrewd and relished. But when the employer goes out at about 9, 12 and 3, it is to make a different kind of agreement. On these occasions there is no haggling. The story describes the labourers as anxious for work[8] and the landowner simply tells them to go to his vineyard and he will pay them 'what is fair'.

Lastly he goes out to hire more workers at about five. There is only one more hour before he must pay and dismiss his workers. The workers he sees in the market now are likely to be desperate for work, for they and their families will be living from hand to mouth and will need that day's pay. He simply tells them to go into the vineyard. This time there is no bargaining and no promise. They'll just have to trust him to treat them fairly.

So here we have three kinds of agreement and five lots of workers, all of whom are certain to have a keen eye for their rights and differentials. An awkward position for an employer: especially a landowner who must keep on reasonably good terms with the local work-force. And it's got to be settled without delay. A good employer pays his people before nightfall, so that they can go home comfortably.[9]

Since, as we are to discover, this employer *is* a good one, he arranges payment when sunset starts. His order to the steward to start by paying the last arrivals and to work backwards wasn't particularly significant (see Note III),[10] though of course it's necessary for the story for the first arrivals not to have been paid and gone off before the last arrivals are paid. The explosion comes, not from the order of payment, but from the last being paid as much as the first.

To some extent it wasn't as unlikely or outrageous a solution to the employer's problem as it might seem. The five hirings make it look as though it was a bumper harvest, and a great occasion like that tends to put us in generous mood! More to the point was the custom for paying the semi-

THE WORKERS IN THE VINEYARD 37

employed. This would have entitled those hired later in the day to something like three-quarters of a denarius anyway. If, as seems very possible, the urgency came from its being a Friday, a good employer would feel particularly obliged to get through the payment quickly, undelayed by haggling with the latecomers, since he would be obliged to see that the workers could get home, light a lamp, and broil a fish before sunset.[11] Certainly the employer had been generous. But only to some of the work-force, and even to them not greatly.

So far, then, except for the nagging suspicion that there is more to it than immediately meets the eye, it was an intriguing story about labour relationships, without offering anything particularly extraordinary or dramatic. The audience would on the whole have felt that those who had worked the whole day had been unjustly treated.

But then the employer gives an explanation of this apparent injustice: 'Have I no right to do what I like on my own estate? Why be envious because I am good?'

It is here that the suspicion that we're being asked to go behind the world of barter becomes a certainty. The first part of the landowner's explanation would have been totally unconvincing. He had reversed the order of payment, which was bound to provoke grievance at an apparent injustice, even though, as we have seen, he may have had legitimate reasons for doing so. But the 'right to do what I like on my own estate' would have cut no ice at all as a legitimate reason. Provocation is *not* one of the rights of ownership!

It was typical of Jesus, the master of story-telling, to finish with a word that abruptly changes the focus of the whole story: 'Why be envious because I am *good*?' Into a tale that for the most part had looked quite ordinary, he casually slips, right at the end, a word that said 'God' to the acute listener.

Just as he had done at the turning point of the Samaritan story, here too he uses an alternative word for the one that summed up for the Jew what they knew God to be: full of 'loving-kindness'. Often in the Old Testament we hear the refrain: 'God is good because his loving-kindness (*hesed*) is ever lasting'. Loving-kindness was what made him good: it was what his goodness consisted of. Utter confidence in that could make Jeremiah see, even in the ruined streets of Jerusalem, a vision of people shouting and rejoicing with delight, and hear the voices of bridegroom and bride, and the singing of those bringing sacrifices rejoicing that 'God is good, for his kindness will never end.' It was the thanksgiving hymn of God's people expressing their delight in their God and in what he was for them.[12]

By using the word 'good' at this point in the story, Jesus was suggesting that his parable was about God's essential characteristic and was inviting his audience to look again at the story.[13]

Who has total freedom 'on his own estate'? Who can claim that goodness is the hallmark of all his actions? Well, God of course. From this standpoint Jesus' listeners might be able to turn back on the story and see the details fitting into place.

The repeated invitations to work in the vineyard: were these God's covenants with people to work with him for reward? Of course it wasn't really many covenants, but *one* covenant: the same agreement and the same reward, but repeated because of the inadequate performance of earlier generations and because God is merciful.

Hadn't the covenant been offered for only one motive: the gracious kindness of one who has total freedom 'on his own estate'?

Jesus wasn't suggesting to his audience anything they didn't already know. They knew that God is merciful and forgiving. In fact their religious leaders taught that even the great heroes of their history, like Abraham, would fail at the judgement if it weren't for God's forgiveness.[14]

But they had allowed that primary truth about our relationship with God to slide into second place. As they had come to see it, a person's duty was to *earn* God's kindness. You put your stack of good deeds on the table. If they came to more than your bad deeds, you had won the contract. God's love wasn't something you'd been given, but something you'd earned. It's obviously true that we're not really accepting God's love for us if it doesn't influence our actions: love without deeds is a hollow pretence. But the rabbis were confusing effect with cause, symptom with the fire that fuels a relationship.

If you didn't see the free gift of generous love as primary, then you couldn't understand Jesus' friendship with 'sinners'. You simply applied the balance-sheet approach, and it seemed obvious in their case that debit soared far above credit. So, like those vineyard-workers, you complained.

'Remember the history of our people,' Jesus is saying here to the grumblers. 'Doesn't my story remind you of it? Doesn't it help you to see that though a real relationship with God (or with anyone!) is impossible if we're not prepared to try to live up to it, its foundation is not our "credits" but God's goodness?'

Surprise or rancour at the different forms in which God might offer his friendship – say to the social outcasts, wasn't that to forget that a covenant with God could not be reduced to the details of a deal about merits or to calculated differentials? Surely the whole point of such a covenant is to offer the *limitless* kindness of God? All are offered this same great gift, you and they, first comers and last, each in his or her own circumstances of life.

The parable was asking Jesus' critics to consider whether, in *that* context, they shouldn't exchange their rancour for a share in his joy.

REFLECTION

1. Jesus, we have seen, starts his story as almost one just about industrial relations (the doubt coming from what a 'subversive' religious teacher like him might be getting at in a story about a vineyard and a series of 'agreements' to work in it). The next stage for his listeners was the realization that this was indeed a topical story: trying to answer the complaints of those who had done 'a heavy day's work in all the heat', while the tax-collectors who had lived irreligious lives were being received as his close friends. Even the story seemed to be confirming the injustice of this – and therefore the falsity of Jesus' apparent claims, for what landowner has the right 'to do what I like on my own estate'? The third

and last stage comes with the last word of the parable. It's like a sombre landscape suddenly being suffused by sunshine. We're brought up sharp against the reality of God and asked to consider whether the evidence of Jesus' life doesn't force us to see the landscape as suffused by that reality and to consider how different that makes everything.

2. We know, just as Jesus' listeners did, that the goodness of God does suffuse the landscape of all people's lives. The parable reminds us how easy it is to know this in theory but to ignore it in practice, because we have never allowed our eyes to be opened to the goodness of God and of people.

3. Today, even in the western world, most people haven't a genuine opportunity of being convinced and committed Christians. In this parable Jesus was claiming to be making yet another in the long series of agreements or 'covenants' with the workers in God's 'vineyard'. What an outrageously 'way-out' kind of covenant it must have seemed! The parable was asking the listeners to consider whether it was in fact outrageous if you took seriously the goodness of God and how God fosters goodness in people and responds lovingly to them. Is the parable asking us too to take a wider view of where God may be especially present? Are we taking a full part in the coming of the Kingdom if we see it, in today's circumstances, only in terms of what Christians are doing? Would that be to accept the parable's very forceful invitation to revise our whole view of how God deals with the people in his 'vineyard' in the light of who he really is? What are the practical implications of this for me where I live?

4. And when we look beyond our immediate environment, don't we also see there evidence of deeply Christian values? A non-Christian report on International Development Issues had two principal motives for its proposals: 'human solidarity and a commitment to international justice'. (*North-South* (The Brandt Report), p. 64★)

★For details of this Report, see footnote on page 19.

NOTES

1. The interest of the story is heightened by three surprises: that the farmer goes out to hire workers five times in one day, the last time when the working day has only one more hour to go; that the last-comers receive a denarius; and, above all, that those who have endured the heat and twelve hours' hard work get no more than the last-comers. By leading up to that culminating surprise the whole story forces the listener to ask: Why were the last-comers so favoured?

In terms of the story itself, the reason given by the farmer is not, we have seen, satisfactory: he was free to be generous to the last-comers if he wanted to be, but not in such a way as to flaunt his favouring them in front of those not so favoured. Recognizing this, some commentators find an alternative explanation in the story itself: the first-comers had shown no trust in the farmer (they had haggled for the terms of their contract), while the others had – especially the last-comers who hadn't even had a promise from him that they would be paid 'a fair wage'. It is this that prompts the farmer's generosity to them.

At the level of *the story*, this seems unconvincing. As one of the advocates of this view himself says: 'At the eleventh hour it was patent to both sides that there was not time left for bargaining. The men still idle were desperate for some money to take home...',[15] and the story gives little weight to the intervening hirings.

At the level of *the message*, we have to be careful. We have seen that our eyes are fully opened to what the parable is saying by the farmer's claim of God-like goodness. The stress of the story is, therefore, more on the farmer's attitude than on what prompts that attitude. The parable is reminding the listener of the ever-repeated generosity of God to his beloved people. On the other hand, it is doing this in terms of Jesus' circumstances. The Pharisees were 'murmuring' against his friendship with the tax-collectors and sinners who by their actions had put themselves *outside* God's agreement with his people. That seemed to entitle them to punishment, not reward; and yet Jesus was so conspicuously favouring them.

So Jesus by his actions was clearly saying that God's offer of covenant or special friendship with men and women was not confined to set terms of agreement, and was especially made to people who loved and trusted him.[16] The last-comers in the story were, through no fault of their own, desperate for help. Although the story suggests that the farmer may have taken them on, not so much out of pity as from the need to get in the harvest, at *parable* level (i.e. in the light of God's *hesed*), Jesus' obvious pity for the socially and religiously dispossessed could well have been suggested.[17]

II. We notice the psychological skill with which Jesus gives a full expression to his objectors' feelings (and his sympathy for how they feel): 'we have done a heavy day's work in all the heat.'[18]

III. The original version would have stopped at verse 15. Some versions add 'Many are called, but few are chosen.' This meant 'although all are called, it doesn't follow that all that number will be chosen.'[19] But all *are* recompensed here. And the best manuscripts don't give the phrase. Nor did 'Thus the last will be first, and the first last' belong to the original parable. Matthew, it is true, presents the whole parable as an explanation of 19: 30, which is taken up at its conclusion though with a somewhat different meaning. But Matthew was using the parable to explain why the gospel message first offered to the Jews had in fact been received by the Gentiles, and it is he who seems to have linked the parable with v. 16. In Aramaic 'beginning with the last' etc. (v. 8) may not mean what he takes it to mean, but 'Pay the workers *including* the last.'[20] In any case, to receive first would have been no real advantage to them; their joy came from being paid so much. The sentence is found elsewhere in the Gospels. It doesn't throw light on the problem raised by the parable: the conduct of the farmer.[21]

THE GREAT SUPPER Matthew 22: 1–10; Luke 14: 15–24

One of those gathered round the tables said to him, 'Happy the man who will be at the feast of the kingdom of God!' But he said to him, 'There was a man who gave a great feast, and he invited a large number of people. When the time for the feast came, he sent his servant to say to those who had been invited, "Come along: everything is ready now." But all alike started to make excuses. The first said, "I have bought a piece of land and must go and see it. Please accept my apologies." Another said, "I have bought five yoke of oxen and am on my way to try them out. Please accept my apologies." Yet another said, "I have just got married and so am unable to come."

The servant returned and reported this to his master. Then the householder, in a rage, said to his servant, "Go out quickly into the streets and alleys of the town and bring in here the poor, the crippled, the blind and the lame." "Sir," said the servant, "your orders have been carried out and there is still room." Then the master said to the servant, "Go to the open roads and the hedgerows and force people to come in to make sure my house is full; because, I tell you, not one of those who were invited shall so much as taste of my dinner." '

For fashionable dinner parties in Jerusalem the custom was that, on the day of the party, a servant would be sent to the people who had been invited to remind them that they were expected that evening.[1] In the party the host of this story had arranged, it was possible that some of the guests might now have to decline, given the large number originally invited. But in any country, one would normally be expected not to decline on the very day of the party. And still more is this the case in the East, where giving and accepting social invitations and gifts are important ways of holding society together.[2]

In fact, *all* of them declined. Such extraordinary unanimity pointed to a deliberate rejection. The guests were spurning the social relationship with the host that the party would have consolidated. Rejected and offended by this social sabotage, the host was furious.

An additional cause for his anger was the kind of excuse given.[3] They were the excuses permitted by the Bible for not taking part in a *war*! More false and insolent excuses for not attending a banquet could hardly have been invented. No wonder he decided there and then that this would be the end of his friendship with these people. A host would send portions of the meal out to those unavoidably absent. After a rejection like this, there would be no question of that. 'Not one of those invited people shall so much as taste of my dinner.'[4]

That was one consequence of the host's anger. The other was to make sure that the banquet was eaten by others. The Jews well understood the obligation of the well-off to help the poor, but that's clearly not what this host is doing. Here he is giving expression to his anger at an affront.[5] Jesus' audience would have sympathized with him. To be let down at the last moment, with excuses like that, by all your social acquaintances, when you had invited them to a great dinner: anyone would be furious!

But, as so often with Jesus' stories, it was clear as he told it that it wasn't as simple as it looked. The allusions it contained made it obvious that Jesus wasn't just telling a harmless anecdote.

First, there was the allusion to what he himself did: he was well known to have parties. Like the man in the story, he feasted with rejects because the 'invited' wouldn't come. Could this have something to do with the Messiah's feast? Jesus' story, after all, seems to have been prompted by a remark by one of his fellow-guests about that feast.[6] And

THE GREAT SUPPER

those excuses connected with war service: well, the Messiah's feast and the Holy War were both images for the coming of God's Kingdom.

As the details of the story fell into place in the listeners' minds, their sense of disturbance would have grown. It was clearly a story about people being 'called' or 'invited'.[7] That was precisely their situation. They were the people who had been called by God: 'I have called you by your name, you are mine.' 'I, God, have called you to serve the cause of right; I have taken you by the hand and formed you; I have appointed you as the covenant of the people and light of the nations, to open the eyes of the blind, to free captives from prison, and those who live in darkness from the dungeon.'[8]

But this story is about 'invited' people who together make the kind of excuse that would lead any reasonable host to anger, and just as it starts with the host 'inviting' them, it ends with his saying that none of the 'invited' 'shall so much as taste of my dinner'.

What drove the point home was the type of people who ate the banquet instead. They were Jews, but the word 'invited' isn't applied to them. And Jesus' audience would well have understood why not. They were the type whom religious people excluded from that category.

It is only in the last few years that we have been able to get close to their way of thinking and hence to pick up this allusion in Jesus' story.[9] At the time of Jesus the community of monks at Qumran, near Jericho, had determined who would *not* be members of God's people when his Kingdom came. Such people would not be – in the word they themselves used – 'the invited'. The Qumran community had lists of what would disqualify such people. You were disqualified if you were 'maimed, blind or lame'. You had instead to be among 'the wise men of the congregation, the understanding and the knowledgeable, the pure in piety, the men of great virtue'. To Qumran members those physical deformities were signs that you couldn't be a 'man of virtue': they proved that you had sinned and were being punished by God.

So in Jesus' story, not only were the invited (through their fault) rejected, but, just as disturbing and shocking, the professionally *dis*qualified took their place.

But everyone knew why the maimed, the blind and the lame were held to be disqualified. Their disabilities were held to be a sign of God's disfavour. People were measuring God's creative and loving generosity by yardsticks like these.

What, then, did Jesus seem to be suggesting? Of course we have to see the story in the context of his life. The main context was the kind of person he was and the open-handed and joyful welcome he showed, especially to those in need. The Kingdom of God wasn't coming in sermons, but in that kind of human action. The purpose of Jesus' parables wasn't to weave together some moral instructions but to help people recognize the significance of what was happening in their midst.

So when Jesus told a story about a feast – *any* kind of feast, you couldn't avoid hearing echoing in the background the laughter of those famous, or notorious, parties of his. You might applaud, or be perplexed, or be angrily indignant at those celebrations of love and healing. You might be open or closed to the possibility that the Kingdom was experienced in their joy. But if this man of controversial feasts and enigmatic parables chose a *feast* as the subject of a story, then it had to conjure up that joy, that welcome, and that openhandedness.

It is particularly necessary to remember this very positive context when we listen to *this* story, because of its negative emphasis. Jesus' feasts were about acceptance; this story is largely about rejection.

In this story Jesus was suggesting that the people whom everyone expected to come to his feast would be excluded and that those whom everyone expected to be excluded would be admitted.

What light does the story throw on the *reasons* for this reversal? We must be careful not to expect a thorough explanation from a simple story. A parable evokes, disturbs and points, rather than explains. But the following seems safe:

1. The 'invited' are rejected through their own fault. The

THE GREAT SUPPER

parable 'works' for its listeners only if we share in the host's anger. It asks us to be indignant about the guests' rejection of the invitation.

But what fault was it that provoked this indignation? That *all* of them refused;[10] or that they gave insultingly inappropriate excuses; or that they gave excuses that showed blindness to the fact that this was the *Messiah's* feast; or that they were making use of Scripture to hide from themselves the great event that Scripture was designed to reveal; or their assumption that they could decline the invitation and yet remain on the invitation list and friends of the host?

It seems to me that all of these possibilities were being put by Jesus to his audience. The motives of his audience were, like those of any group of people, complex and various. The story was intended to help some of Jesus' self-complacent fellow-diners to consider theirs.

2. What reasons are suggested for the other side of the reversal: the summoning of *other* people to the feast?

We are told two things about this summoning. First, it is universal in scope: the *town* in the first sending of the servant and the *country* in the second. And we are told secondly that the people summoned were 'the poor, the crippled, the blind and the lame'. The last three epithets denoted them, as we have seen, as the people whose handicaps were taken as showing that they weren't God's elect. The first epithet, 'the poor', was suggestively ambiguous. It could, like the other epithets, refer to people suffering from handicaps or it could refer to the people of God as the *destitute* nation befriended by God who must always care for the poor and powerless, in order to fulfil their vocation.[11]

By inserting the word 'poor' into the list, Jesus was reminding them that God's love went especially to those in need. By mentioning 'the crippled, the blind and the lame', he would have been understood to allude, not just to the needy, but to people who were excluded by some at least of his contemporaries from the Kingdom because of a Scripture text on ritual purity.[12]

He was asking his audience to see his notorious friends above all as people in need: as people whom God would particularly love. They were 'the poor' to whom he had been commissioned to bring the good news. He was asking them to see beyond self-regarding, unfeeling, legalistic pettiness and recognize the love and joy and healing in their midst.

REFLECTION

1. Jesus saw what he is offering us in terms of a feast. Like any great poet he used symbols to convey his meaning when it was too rich, too profound, for precise description. The symbol of a feast offers our imagination many avenues to explore. We may like to think of the Last Supper. Or we may remind ourselves of the splendour and shared joy of an oriental feast, like the one where the rich man 'invites his friends to eat with him, and they come and speak with one another before the palace, joyfully awaiting his feast, the enjoyment of good things, of great wealth and joy and happiness.' Jesus' listeners knew that God's full coming through the Messiah had long been pictured as a feast for all peoples at which they would say, 'See, this is our God in whom we hoped for salvation; God is the one in whom we hoped. We exult and we rejoice that he has saved us' (Isaiah 25: 8–9).

2. Pharisees couldn't recognize Jesus in his 'breaking bread' with people who needed his love. They couldn't recognize the coming of the Messiah in shared joy and human warmth and support when they saw it. They were certain that *they* were the 'invited' people, the 'religious' people. What prevented them recognizing the Messiah who had come among them? Can the same things make people blind to Jesus' presence amongst us today? To what extent are we afflicted by this blindness? What can cure it: reflection, discussion, experience, or a combination of these?

3. We need to try to understand things, to chart reasons and consequences and the structure of events. So we have to lay them out in our minds in categories. But the parable shows us how disastrous it is if we confine God's approach, which bypasses all categories and goes straight to the person as

someone needing love and wanting friendship and support. As the community whose task is to embody Jesus for the world today, do we need to be more willing to come out of the shelter of the categories we've become familiar with and model ourselves more on his approach? Do some of our accustomed ways of seeing people and things obliterate our feeling for that immediate response to human need and affection that people saw in Jesus and which is reflected in this parable?

4. 'Few people in the North have any detailed conception of the extent of poverty in the Third World or of the forms that it takes. Many hundreds of millions of people in the poorer countries are preoccupied solely with survival and elementary needs. For them work is frequently not available or, when it is, pay is very low and conditions barely tolerable. Homes are constructed of impermanent materials and have neither piped water nor sanitation. Electricity is a luxury. Health services are thinly spread and in rural areas only rarely within walking distance. Primary schools, where they exist, may be free and not too far away, but children are needed for work and cannot easily be spared for schooling. Permanent insecurity is the condition of the poor. There are no public systems of social security in the event of unemployment, sickness or death of a wage-earner in the family. Flood, drought or disease affecting people or livestock can destroy livelihoods without hope of compensation. In the North, ordinary men and women . . . rarely face anything resembling the total deprivation found in the South.' (*North-South* (The Brandt Report), p. 49*)

---

*For details of this Report, see footnote on page 19.

THE TWO SONS   Matthew 21: 28–31

'A man had two sons. He went to the first and said, "My boy, go and work today in the vineyard." "I will, sir", the boy replied; but he never went. The father came to the second and said the same. "I will not", he replied, but afterwards he changed his mind and went. Which of these two did as his father wished?' 'The second', they said. Then Jesus said, 'I tell you solemnly that tax collectors and prostitutes are entering the Kingdom of God rather than you.'[1]

The elder brother plainly falls into a snare that can beset us all. He gets drugged by his own fine phrases. If you ask me whether I love my neighbour and want justice for the underprivileged, I'll sincerely tell you that I do. Those fine ideals are an essential part of my philosophy.

So too with the elder brother. Work in the vineyard was an essential part in *his* philosophy. It was, after all, the source of the family's livelihood. The father asked him to go as his 'son'. Respect for his father and his rights as owner would have seemed to him noble, natural and traditional.

But when it came to putting his philosophy into practice, the prospect of a long day of hard work under the scorching sun could have been distinctly unattractive. So he failed to turn up.

The younger son had taken the opposite course. In fiction and fact younger sons can be rebellious or non-conformist, in order to assert their independence. So, not unexpectedly, this one began by refusing his father's request. But later he thought better of it and went, and so gained his father's approval.

This homely, everyday occurrence was intended to help Jesus' audience understand what was happening among them. The 'religious' people prayed every sabbath in their local synagogue for the coming of the Kingdom. If you had

THE TWO SONS 51

even hinted to them that their prayer was insincere, they would have been hurt and uncomprehending. *Of course* they wanted the Kingdom! Why else were they Jews? Why else did they put up with physical hardships like the weekly fasts, or financial loss in giving up a tenth of their income? How absurd even to ask whether they were sincere!

Yet the fact remained that the *reality* of the Kingdom, when it came in Jesus, was too tough for them. The toughness was subtler and much more demanding than the labour and heat of a day's work in the vineyard. It meant trusting God so much that you would put at risk all the categories and accustomed ways in which you managed your life. The security and satisfaction that came from long-known landmarks would go. And instead you had, what?

It is here that we really need to try to form a picture of what the people who were open to Jesus actually saw. He was clearly someone who befriended others in a quite exceptional way. The Gospel accounts offer no more than sketches, but it's not difficult to fill in the picture. They tell us that he dined with tax collectors and sinners. Was this just a matter of noble condescension, like a president of a big company occasionally taking a meal in his or her workers' canteen – surrounded no doubt by personal aides and other executives?

We don't have to guess the answer. One of the most certain things we know about Jesus is that for him, like his compatriots, a meal was the profoundest expression of fellowship. Do you remember the last time someone offered real fellowship to you? Words were probably used; but far more important may have been the physical signs (a handshake, a kiss, a smile) that conveyed to you that this wasn't just words, but that the whole person was *for* you.

That is clearly what people saw in Jesus' meals. The smile, the concern, the unassuming comradeship, the shared happiness. He was totally *there*: his whole personality was *for* you, saying OK to your 'story' with his look and his actions. It was like this whoever you were and whatever you'd done, provided you were at least interested in being like him: someone really open to human life in its depth and its demands.

That is really all there was to see in Jesus. Then as now, religious people found difficulty in accepting that *this* is where we can find the Kingdom. Religion can involve us, as it did many Jews, in a good deal of self-sacrifice, all the way from getting up early on Sundays to forgoing a lucrative deal of doubtful morality. The parable is meant to remind us that just as the Pharisees became so deafened by their affirmation of religion that they couldn't recognize a real relationship with God when they saw one, so *we* can become so deafened by our affirmation of religion that it becomes a substitute for, or even an unconscious insurance against, Jesus himself.

Jesus, it reminds us, is there *with people*. It is by sharing with him in that that we find the Kingdom. Like working a twelve-hour shift in a vineyard, we often find that hard. But when we allow this parable to jog our memory, we realize what the work consists of and perhaps glimpse the joy of doing it.

Isn't it true that the most striking difference in our experience of the families we know is that between parents who try to make their children like themselves and those who try to appreciate the unique qualities of each and help each become his or her true self? If the local Christian communities can become as eager to learn *the real needs* of those around them and respond as lovingly, then we shall have heard and accepted the message of this parable.[2]

REFLECTION

1. The most admired religious people of the day being accused of really saying 'No' to God! What a monstrous slander!

The parable forces us to ask whether religious people today can deceive themselves in the same way as the Pharisees. A large part of the reason why *they* couldn't recognize a quite special presence of God in Jesus was that they had inherited from many generations a very limited understanding of God. That understanding had become so deeply embedded in the institution of Pharisaism and in general attitudes that it had become an accepted part of the landscape.

Have we, like the Pharisees, inherited a tradition of being able to recognize God, in practice, mainly in our church, or even just in 'our kind of people'? In that way, God becomes a tame God, who almost 'belongs' to us. Tragic self-deception, the parable says. What do we need to do, as individuals and as members of our churches, to avoid that where we live today? The Pharisees would have needed a fundamentally different outlook. To what extent is that true of us?

2. 'Jesus' "lack of moral principles". He sat at meal with publicans and sinners, he consorted with harlots. Did he do this to obtain their votes? Or did he think that perhaps he could convert them by such "appeasement"? Or was his humanity rich and deep enough to make contact, even in them, with that in human nature which is common to all

men and women, indestructible, and upon which the future has to be built?' (Dag Hammarskjöld, *Markings*, tr. W.H. Auden (London 1964), p. 134).

NOTES

I. Here we have a simple, homely story, with its clear-cut conclusion in verse 31. It is true that this story lacks the vivid, realistic details that Jesus' stories tend to have. But this kind of comparison with closely observed family and economic life; the central point it makes about the coming of the Kingdom through Jesus' relationship with people; and Jesus' typical way of backing what he said with 'Amen, I say to you' (together probably with the elder son/younger son contrast on the same lines as in the Prodigal Son parable): all these suggest that in verses 28–31 we have at least an outline of a parable by Jesus.

It is true that many of the words and phrases used in these verses are typical of Matthew.[3] As we shall see in a moment, Matthew modified the parable in order to apply it to a major problem facing the Church of his time.[4] As we see from the other two parables from this part of his Gospel (the *Wicked Husbandmen* and the *Great Supper*), he had no hesitation in doing so and in freely rewriting the original parable for that purpose. As we see in the Great Supper parable, he felt free to omit many details of the original, which may help to explain this parable's lack of colour.

II. Jesus was using this parable, as he did that of the Prodigal Son, to try to help the religious people see what was happening and change their minds. His picture of that easily recognizable contrast between two kinds of attitude was a kind of mirror in which they might see themselves and understand *why* he was so scandalously giving 'preference' to the despised.

Matthew's approach is less gentle. When he added verse 32[5] and placed the whole passage in the context of 23–7, the fact that the original story was a carefully calculated invitation to change one's mind was of less interest to him. What he was conscious of was that the Jewish religious leaders had now for decades resisted both Christ and the Church. He wanted to make clear why they were not responding to the authority of Christ's Church: because even before Jesus, even in John the Baptist whom their own followers had recognized to be a prophet and 'a pattern of true righteousness',[6] they had turned their backs on the evidence of God's pres-

THE TWO SONS

ence among them. He wasn't interested here, as the parable had been, in suggesting that we find the Kingdom of God, if at all, in our sharing in God's work for the physically or morally disadvantaged, but in the tragedy of a long-standing resistance to their God of his own people. And of course the fact that the original parable was about a vineyard made it particularly suitable for his purpose.[7]

III. For Matthew the rejection of John the Baptist by the Jewish authorities was of great importance. Matthew regarded the murder of John as a proof of their guilt. It was a typical case, for Matthew, of a disobedient Israel rejecting a prophet God had sent to them.[8] Matthew was 'concerned with presenting the entire process of the history of Israel whose leaders had always been false. . . . In this case, they had failed to acclaim the Messiah and had brought final disaster upon the nation.'[9]

In these six stories Jesus tried to help his listeners understand what they saw him doing. If they looked at Jesus' actions in the light of their experience of God and of the promises he had made to them, might a feeling of doubt and even of scandal turn into joy?

In these stories it's impossible to draw the line between God and Jesus. In the *Prodigal Son* story, who is the father meant to remind us of: God or Jesus? The younger son expresses his decision to go back to his father in words that were reminiscent of Israel's turning back to God in Hosea's prophecy; the very image of father would have suggested God in that context (Hosea 11: 1–4). Yet the story was clearly about the different reactions of people to Jesus.

The story of the *Workers in the Vineyard* inevitably reminded the listeners that they were God's vineyard and of the agreements that God had made with them about this down the centuries. Yet the whole point of the story was to ask whether *Jesus* hadn't the right to make one more in that series of agreements or 'covenants' between God and his people. 'Have I no right to do what I like on my own estate? Why be envious because I am good?' was the evocative conclusion, for his listeners knew whom that last word, 'good', suggested. Was there evidence that Jesus had, in a quite special way, the 'goodness', lovingkindness and faithfulness of God, so that *he* had the right to make 'covenants'?

Then who was the shepherd who was seeking to gather together his flock? Jesus' listeners knew the prophecies and still spoke of God as the Shepherd of Israel who would one day gather again the scattered flock. But the parable would 'work' for the listener in explaining Jesus' actions only if he or she would recognize that that gathering was taking place before their eyes.

In the *Great Supper* story, which helped to make the outrageous suggestion that those scandalous meals of Jesus were to do with the full coming of God that had long been pictured as a meal, who was deciding who should and who should not be invited? And could one for a moment accept the implication of the parable of the *Two Sons* that in saying 'No' to Jesus one was really saying 'No' to God?

CHAPTER 3 What Happens Now?

The Mustard Seed *and* the Leaven
The Seed Growing Secretly
The Tares *and* the Dragnet
The Sower

Suppose you came to accept the evidence that Jesus' stories were trying to help you understand. Then you might join him in some way. But what did you find yourself involved in? Some might ask: Where *is* this Kingdom of God? What is there to show for all those impressive promises?

Apart from the healings, whose impact may have vanished quickly, there remained a profoundly distrusted man and a usually unimpressive group of followers.

Through his stories about the *Mustard Seed* and the *Leaven*, Jesus spoke with humour about his own position in all this, and through the parable on the *Seed Growing Secretly* about ours.

Those who stayed with Jesus, in spite of discouragement, needed help to understand what following him involves. In the stories of the *Sower*, the *Tares* and the *Dragnet* Jesus encourages us to reflect on the opportunity that brings and on the importance of our basic decisions about ourselves.

THE MUSTARD SEED   Mark 4: 30–2; Matthew 13: 31f; Luke 13: 18f

'What is the Kingdom of God like, and to what shall I compare it? It is like a grain of mustard seed, which a man took and sowed in his field, and it grew and became a tree, and the birds of the air made nests in its branches.'[1]

THE LEAVEN   Matthew 13:33; Luke 13: 20f

'The Kingdom of God is like the yeast a woman took and mixed in with three measures of flour till it was leavened all through.'

These parables express Jesus' astonished delight that in him, an ordinary man, the Kingdom of God was being offered. The supremely desirable was in the gift of himself and his friends.

Both parables begin with something that is extremely unimpressive or contemptible. A mustard seed was proverbially the smallest of all seeds, and leaven tended to suggest corruption and the religiously impure.[2] Both end with marvellously different pictures: a bush twice the height of a man or woman, and enough bread for one hundred people. What would have struck the oriental mind in these two sets of contrasting situations would have been 'not growth but miracle, not organic and biological development but the giftlike nature, the graciousness and the surprise of the ordinary.'[3]

Jesus seems to be expressing what he felt not only by contrast. He was also using some easily recognizable allusions. So his leaven story ends with 'three measures of meal'.[4] This seems to indicate more than just a very large quantity. Three-measure baking in the Old Testament suggested a special manifestation of God. When God visited Abraham by the oaks of Mamre, he told his wife to knead 'three measures of fine meal and make loaves' (Genesis 18:6). When Gideon met God at the oak of Ophrah, Gideon prepared unleavened cakes with an ephah (three measures) of flour (Judges 6:19).[5]

So in his story of the leaven Jesus is seeing his situation not just in terms of an extraordinary contrast between the beginning and the end of making bread: he is also seeing it in terms of something comic and crucial. My fellow-outcasts and I, he's saying, the 'leaven' or corruption of society as we're thought to be: how extraordinary and how marvellous that hiddenly[6] in us is that special manifestation of God we call his 'Kingdom'!

Once we have recognized the tone of comic irony in the *Leaven* parable, it is much easier to interpret that of the *Mustard Seed*.[7]

It ends by evoking one of the most magnificent scenes in the Old Testament. It was painted by the prophet Ezekiel.[8] After vividly showing how Israel's reliance on mere political manoeuvre will lead it to disaster, it tells of how God will eventually restore Israel to splendid life. How better typify such a life than by the great cedar trees on Mount Lebanon:

> From the top of the cedar,
> from the highest branch I will take a shoot
> and plant it myself on a very high mountain of Israel.
> It will sprout branches and bear fruit,
> and become a noble cedar.
> Every kind of bird will live beneath it,
> every winged creature rest in the shade of its branches,
> and every tree of the field will learn that I, God, am the one,
> who stunts tall trees and makes the low ones grow,
> who withers green trees and makes the withered green.
> I, God, have spoken, and I will do it.
> (Ezekiel 17: 22–4)

Here again Jesus' story points to a comic contrast. Here is what everyone considers unimpressive: an untrained, disloyal Jew who went around with the riff-raff of society. But in what's happening in *us*, Jesus is saying, we experience God's planting of that mighty cedar which will give a home to the birds. Now we can tell through our own experience that God is 'one who stunts tall trees and makes the low ones grow'.

REFLECTION

These two brief stories read like rapidly tossed-off asides to Jesus' friends: off-the-cuff comments on life. Their mood is of eagerness and delight. The Kingdom is no remote, pompous event, but you can sense it everywhere. All around us are events that seem humdrum, and people who seem unimpressive. Why not take another look? Jesus invites us.

But it isn't just the superb assurance that the Kingdom is really in life as we know it, growing in all that ordinariness to a cedar-like outcome. A fanatic might have said the same.

But a fanatic lacks that feeling for real life that we see in Jesus' stories, and perhaps especially in these. A fanatic sees life running along a metal track; Jesus saw it running through the contrasts, disappointments, compromises, surprises that our everyday lives are full of.

Jesus knew all about the tragedy in human life – especially that of the lost opportunity. His lament over Jerusalem that insisted on remaining deaf to his call makes that plain to us. But in his stories of the *Mustard Seed* and the *Leaven* he shows us that even in frustration and rebuff he saw the optimism and merriment of the Kingdom.

NOTES

What was Jesus trying to do in these parables? There seem to be three possible answers:

I. Jesus is presenting us in each case with an entirely unimpressive beginning, like the mustard seed (proverbially the smallest) and a marvellously different picture: a bush twice the height of a man or woman, and enough bread for one hundred people. By this contrast we experience not 'growth but miracle, not organic and biological development but the gift-like nature, the graciousness and the surprise of the ordinary'. It expressed Jesus' own experience of just such a miracle of God's full presence and power (his 'Kingdom') in his own entirely unimpressive circumstances.

II. The focus isn't on the *contrast* between two sharply juxtaposed pictures but on the *slow, secret growth* between the start of each process and its end. It expresses not so much the surprise, delight and wonder at an astonishing gift, but a feeling of reassurance. Small and unimpressive things *do* grow into great things. They seem not even to be present, but they are nevertheless there, gradually achieving their great promise.

III. The third possibility is that the climax of these two stories isn't just a 'miracle' of nature, but expresses the presence of God, since they both allude to Old Testament texts that refer to that.

Obviously these three possibilities overlap to a large extent. The third is more a development of the others than a different option: it deepens the feeling of God's climactic presence in what is being pointed to. In each of them the parable is about the presence of God in Jesus' activity, and in each there are two very different stages. Nevertheless there are important differences between I and II. The first is mainly concerned with astonished delight at God's Kingdom being present now; the second with reassurance about the certainty of its coming.

Although the second of these possibilities has often been proposed, it seems unlikely to represent what Jesus was saying, since in such a story the oriental mind wouldn't have been interested in the process of growth but in the paradox of two fundamentally different situations.

To understand this parable, we need to try to stand where Jesus stood. Like him, we can experience the wonder of God's presence in the unimpressive. What else, after all, is the life of a Christian? But how flat and insipid it can become if we aren't aware of that paradox! If I don't see it as astonishing gift, I'm not really seeing it at all. Instead it will either mean nothing to me, or it will be something that stifles or burdens me, and so it will be a caricature of its true self.

THE SEED GROWING SECRETLY
Mark 4: 26–9

'This is what the kingdom of God is like. A man throws seed on the land. Night and day, while he sleeps, when he is awake, the seed is sprouting and growing; how he does not know. In some marvellous and mysterious way the land produces first the shoot, then the ear, then the full grain in the ear. But, *immediately* the crop is ripe he plies the sickle: because harvest-time has come.'[1]

Those who believe in Jesus have always been faced with the problem that this parable tries to solve: we believe that Jesus is present among us inaugurating the Kingdom of God; but what is there to show for it?

Life goes on in its humdrum way. In the chores, the responsibilities, and the occasional successes of life, where is there evidence for such a tremendous event as the coming of God's full power and presence? Can we really say that his Kingdom is breaking in upon us through Jesus' presence as he so clearly asserted, or have we been deceived?

We have grown so accustomed to the lack of dramatic signs of God's presence that it is easy to become immune to the problem. 'The Kingdom of God' may become for us just a vague religious cliché. If it becomes that, we shall no longer *expect* it to mean anything very distinctive in our lives. In that way the problem vanishes, and with it the main significance for us of Jesus' message.

But if we do expose ourselves to that message, the problem is bound to strike us. Then we share the problem as Jesus' contemporaries faced it as they listened to this parable. They, of course, still had the voice of John the Baptist ringing in their ears to remind them of the imminence and dramatic force of the Kingdom. 'Even now', he had proclaimed, 'the axe is laid to the roots of the trees.' This rugged and tempestuous prophet insisted that 'the one who follows me is more powerful than I am', because he was to be God's supreme intervention into human history. In another typically dramatic image, he had told them that 'his winnowing-fan is in his hand; he will clear his threshing-floor and gather his wheat into the barn' (Matthew 3: 10–12). And Jesus himself stressed the *urgency* of the need to repent.

But after all that, what happened? People were healed and befriended; some puzzling stories were told. But the enemies of the Kingdom remained in power, and life went on much the same as before. After that stupendous announcement, nothing. So Jesus told a story to help his followers understand the new situation.

As so often in Jesus' parables, the ending provides the clue to what it is trying to say. The first two-thirds of the parable are relaxed, laconic, and apparently ordinary. A farmer throws seed on the earth and then doesn't bother about it. Nature takes its course. Then abruptly the rhythm changes. There is a rattle of words suggesting contrast and speed. 'But, *immediately* the crop is ripe he plies the sickle: because harvest-time has come.'

So, after lassitude, a sudden climax. But what a climax! That sentence sets up the final grand scenario long awaited by the Jews. It is a deliberate quotation from Joel's prophecy of the coming of God for the great judgement:

> Let the nations rouse themselves, . . .
> for I am going to sit in judgement . . .
> on all the nations round.
> Put the sickle in:
> the harvest is ripe.
> (Joel 4: 12–13)

Now the parable is clearly *not* saying: God's great act of judgement will come. That was already known. It was showing *the relationship between two points*: the *present* situation of Jesus' original listeners and any of us who hear the parable today and *that judgement*. That relationship, it tells us, is just like the relationship shown in the story. So let's look more carefully at how its two sections relate to each other.

As we have already seen, the story starts quietly and

THE SEED GROWING SECRETLY

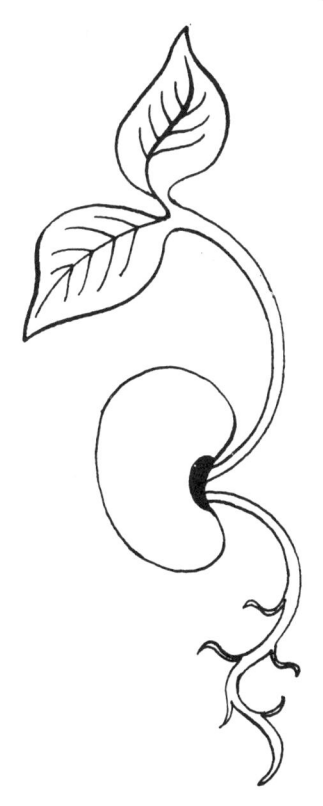

slowly. It begins with what was, for Jesus' audience, an everyday occurrence: a farmer throwing seed on his land; and the Greek presents this as a quick action that the story gets out of the way before settling down to the period of growth. Once that preliminary action is over, we get a contrast between the detailed concentration on the gradual growth of the seed (as many as eight stages are indicated) and the farmer's abandonment of an active part. Apparently completely detached, he continues his day-to-day existence. Then there is a climax. In the Greek there is a sharp-sounding word meaning 'without any recognizable cause'. It suggests that the process we're watching is wonderful: caused by God himself. By placing this word (*automate*) at the most conspicuous place in the first section of the parable, it strongly suggests that the reason for the farmer's apparent detachment was that God, in his marvellous way, was seeing to the growth of the crop: 'In some marvellous and mysterious way, the land produces first the shoot, then the ear, then the full grain in the ear.'

Then the abrupt contrast of the climax: immediately the crop is ripe, the man who had let things be springs into action. His sickle is out, and harvest-time is here.

Jesus is clearly comparing this with the way that God acts: just as a farmer seems completely detached when the seeds he sowed are growing, though in fact he's just waiting for the right moment before he'll be in the very thick of harvest-time, so God may seem completely detached, while in fact he is just waiting for the ripeness for his great intervention.

If we look closely we see that the parable is doing much more than telling us not to worry because God *will* act – important though that is. It's telling us less about the future than about what's happening among us now. Now that Jesus has come we're all involved in a process that is moving towards complete ripeness, and with ripeness the full coming of God's power. Jesus has placed us on the threshold of a new age, and we must become ripe for the harvesting that will introduce it.

But the fact that nothing dramatic seems to happen at such a momentous point isn't strange, isn't really a problem: in fact it's just what you'd expect when a process like that is going on. It points, not to the conclusion that God's Kingdom *isn't* coming but to the conclusion that it is, because that's just how processes like that *do* happen.

REFLECTION

1. Each of us knows a variety of people and gradually we learn more about their ambitions, their motives, their qualities and defects, as well as about our own. Sometimes we ask: what's happening here? Does this endless array of trial and error, success and failure, amount to anything? The Bible says: 'Yes, there'll be a harvest.'

So it's asking us to look afresh at the people we know and

at ourselves with a picture of a harvest in our minds, letting that picture gradually colour our view of our lives.

Growth may be among our first thoughts: that life is about growing towards ripeness. I think about people I know who have a great richness in their humanity – an old man, especially, with a remarkable spirit of joy and trust and love. And then I realize how many of the people I know are struggling, sometimes against great difficulty of temperament or anxiety or some other obstacle, towards a degree of ripeness, and that the Bible is underwriting their efforts and saying to us, 'Yes, that's what is really going on here: ordinary people with ordinary difficulties and opportunities are trying in the middle of all that to achieve ripeness.'

Or we may be more aware that it is shown as *God's* harvest. 'In some marvellous and mysterious way' God is bringing to their fulfilment all men and women who are trying to live good lives. John's Gospel reminds us how immediate and joyful this is (4: 34–6). Matthew stresses that though the harvest is rich, our efforts are needed (9: 37). And the prophecy of Joel quoted in the parable focuses on the importance of what we become through all this: the harvest is the time when wheat is separated from weeds.

2. Above all, Jesus is trying to help us see that we live in a critical time of great promise. 'I've come, and still things look ordinary, uneventful. But my coming means we're on the threshold of harvest time.'

In my circumstances of life what are my opportunities to enter into this great common work in which God and his Church asks us to join him? What needs to be done to give the life around me a sense of the joy and fruitfulness of harvest-time, rather than of something of no lasting significance, and perhaps dreary and sad?

NOTE

The interpretation of this parable obviously depends on the view one takes as to what element in this story is being stressed. If the story is focusing on *what happens to the seed*, then the Kingdom of God is being compared to its growth and the eventual harvest, and it is helping us to realize that the Kingdom grows gradually or that the harvest will eventually come. If the story is focusing on *the sower*, then the Kingdom of God is being compared to his inactivity while the corn is growing, or to his intervention at the time of the harvest, and the comparison may be throwing light on what God or Jesus was doing, or on what the disciples or others should do or think.

It seems possible to find one's way among this confusing array of choices if some features of the story are noted. First, the emphasis in the first section is not on the fact that the seed was sown, or that it grew, but that grew *without the further participation of the farmer*. Second, the function of the second section is evidently to form a contrast with the first section, and must be there to show that the sudden and decisive activity of the farmer at the harvest follows in spite of his lack of activity during that long process of eight stages of growth. Since the description of the harvest is a clear allusion to the coming of the Kingdom at the judgement (cf. Revelation 14: 14–16), the parable must be about the Kingdom.

It seems to follow that although the parable certainly wants us to be aware that the seed is growing towards ripeness and harvest, its particular contribution is to help us see that this growth and its final outcome *are consistent with apparent inactivity on the part of the sower and harvester*. Applied to the situation in Jesus' life-time, it is offering reassurance that in spite of appearances, the Kingdom will come with the suddenness and joyful triumph of a harvest when Jesus' work towards our growth has achieved ripeness. The apparent inactivity is only to be expected in such a process. But look: in Jesus' work, then as now, our growth towards ripeness is moving towards its climax. We can join in it with confident hope.

THE TARES **Matthew 13: 24–30**

'It is with the Kingdom of God as with a man who sowed seed in his field. But when it bore fruit, then also weeds became evident. And in the time of harvest he said to the reapers, "Collect up the weeds so that they may be burnt, but gather together the wheat into my barn." '

THE DRAGNET Matthew 13: 47–48

'It is the case with the coming of the Kingdom of God as with a dragnet cast into the sea that brings in a haul of all kinds. When it is full, the fishermen haul it ashore; then, sitting down, they collect the good ones in a basket and throw away those that are no use.'[1]

Here Jesus offers us two snapshots from everyday life in Galilee. In the first we see a farmer sowing his field with corn. It bears fruit. Weeds naturally grow up amidst the corn. The kind described here (known to botanists as *lolium temulentum*) looks the same as the corn until near the time of harvest. Then at harvest-time the reaper cuts the corn with his sickle, and lets the weeds fall so that they may be gathered into bundles. The harvest of corn will bring joy and a livelihood. The bundles of weeds will be dried so that they will provide fuel in this forest-less country.[2]

Isn't it the same, Jesus asks, with the Kingdom of God? Yes, there is a sowing: you've experienced that for yourselves in what you've seen of me. And this will lead to the joy of a great harvest. This indeed is what the process you're involved in is like. But remember that harvest means selection. The field may all *look* like corn. How important to make sure that you really are 'corn'!

It's worth noticing what Jesus does *not* say in this parable. The Rabbis would have painted ferocious pictures of the last judgement,[3] just as Matthew does with the wicked thrust into the blazing furnace there to weep and grind their teeth. Jesus does not wave threats of terrible punishments over his audience. He's not saying, like an angry school teacher, 'Do this, or else!' He is simply offering us his help in drawing the obvious conclusions from the nature of the process we're involved in. The Kingdom of God is here. The whole world is coming to fruition. Since this is happening through *people*, and especially ourselves, everyone has to say 'Yes' or 'No' to this. Wheat or weed? Being human involves that choice.

Jesus' deliberate rejection of the usual threats of last-judgement wrath helps to bring the focus of the parable much more towards the present. So much of the force of his words and his actions was to declare that in a very real sense the Kingdom is now. For me the Kingdom is what I do about him. Do I respond to his invitation to make this God's world or not?

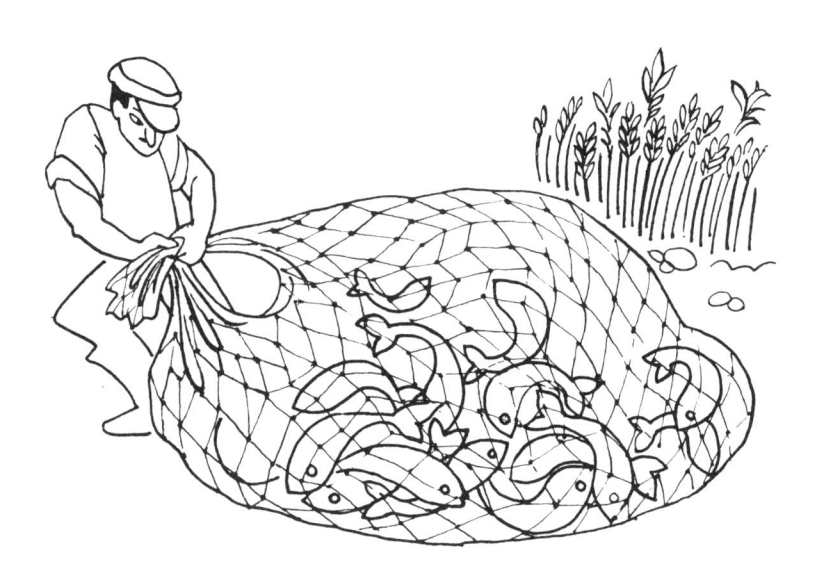

Typical of Jesus, too, is the lack of any attempt to list 'do's' and 'don'ts'. He's not imposing a set of rules; he's asking me to consider my fundamental standpoint. *We* don't judge the people we really know merely by their actions but by the kind of people they seem to be trying to become. Are they trying to be 'good' people, or are they interested only in their own pleasures? And the same with ourselves. I am unlikely to choose to be a bad person. The real test as to what kind of person I am is whether I will make, and maintain, in spite of endless difficulties and failures, my choice to be good. And that means in practice, now that Christ has come, choosing whether to join with him and all his fellow-workers in the growth towards harvest, or letting the opportunity slip, letting my vocation to be human slip, and so losing all touch with 'harvest'; becoming 'weed'.

Jesus' other snapshot was just as recognizable. The warm water and flavour of the Galilean shore of the lake of Genesareth made it full of fish, and fishing an important industry for that province. There were three main kinds of nets used for fishing, each of which we find referred to in the Gospels. The biggest of these was the dragnet, five metres wide and about two hundred and fifty metres long. To possess this giant net was every fisherman's dream. For most fishermen it was too expensive to own, though a group of them might buy one. Then, as now (for such nets are still used), this vast stretch of netting is slung either between two boats or between a boat and the shore, with the upper side held at the surface by corks and the lower side weighted so that it sweeps along the bottom of what has to be a quite shallow and sandy stretch of water. The ends are gradually drawn in until the whole net is brought up on the beach, carrying with it all the fish in the area through which it has passed.

So dragnet-fishing means a catch that is unselective, and, in the kind of water known to Galileans, huge. Once the fish have been dragged onto the shore, selection is obviously necessary. The 'good' ones are gathered into basins or containers, while the rest are left on the shore or dumped back into the sea.[4]

Once again, therefore, Jesus asks us to compare the effect of the coming of the Kingdom with the joy and triumph of a great 'harvest'. Hard work and team effort bring exceptional success.

But not all the fish make up the triumph. Again it's not a question of punishment, but of the kind of fish they are. Fish have no power to choose this. But we, as human beings, do.

THE DRAGNET

REFLECTION

1. Again it is worth reflecting on the 'backdrop' of these parables. A harvest and a dragnet-sized catch of fish were experiences that Jesus' audience were familiar with. We can imagine the sense of being involved with our friends or partners in those activities. Do we sufficiently see the Kingdom as involving us in that kind of activity? Or is it rather a joyless, passive affair where we stay more or less on the sidelines? What would help us be more involved? Are there barriers in ourselves, or in institutions, or in general attitudes? If so, what can we do to help change these?

2. Jesus told these parables to help his friends see that it isn't enough to be with him. When we think about it we realize that that must be so: the purpose of the Kingdom is that we become as fully developed human beings as we are capable of being. But we find it easier to forget and take refuge in mere activity or in a vague sense of belonging to Jesus. Yes, Jesus is saying, the Kingdom is about joy and activity and belonging and achievement. But a mere surface commitment is useless, as the long-term result must show.

3. 'The world can become stronger by becoming a just and humane society. If it fails in this, it will move towards its own destruction.' (*North-South* (the Brandt Report), p. 33*)

NOTES

I. The original parable of the *Tares* gave a picture of everyday farming life, but it is has been changed into an allegory in order to express a different point.[5] The main elements that were added to the original parable were the intervention of the 'enemy', the servants' question about the origin of the weeds, and the dialogue between the 'master' and 'lord' and his 'servants'. We can tell that the first element was absent from the original parable because there the focus was on the ultimate fate of the weeds, not on their origin. The second element wouldn't have fitted into the original parable,

*For details of this Report, see footnote on page 19.

because in ordinary farming life there wouldn't have been anything odd about the appearance of weeds among any harvest! The third element clearly represents a later development, where the 'reapers' have become 'servants' and 'a man' has become 'master' and 'lord': that is, the Church in Matthew's time is listening to the risen Lord's teaching.[6] In *Matthew's* version the parable is a plea for patience: the time for rooting out the weeds is not yet come, though come it certainly will at the judgement. In *Jesus'* version it would be: examine yourself: are you bearing fruit or not? How urgent to do this before the Kingdom comes in its full power!

II. Matthew, as we have just seen, uses Jesus' parable of the *Tares* to help his readers understand why the Christian community comprised both good and bad members.[7] They would have needed that help because it was widely expected at the time that God's people would *not* be a mixture of good and bad, but a 'pure' community. Matthew's answer is that one has to remember two things: first, that Satan ('the enemy') is still powerful; and second, that the judgement is not yet come. He gives this answer through his adaptations of Jesus' parable and through the subsequent interpretation (vv. 36–43). In that interpretation we are shown *two* stages of Jesus' activity. He, 'the Son of Man', through his human nature and that of his followers, sows the good seed. But *at a later stage* he will be the God-like judge. Only at that later stage will his Church be a pure one, with its impure elements erased.

THE SOWER   Mark 4: 3–9; Luke 8: 5–8; Matthew 13: 4–9

'A sower is going out to sow. Now it happens that, as he sows, some of the seed falls on the edge of the path, and the birds come and eat it up. Some seed falls on rocky ground where it finds little soil and springs up straightaway, because there is no depth of earth; and when the sun comes up it is scorched and, not having any roots, it withers away. Some seed falls into thorns, and the thorns grow up and choke it, and it produces no crop. And some seeds fall into rich soil and, growing tall and strong, produce crop; and yield thirty, sixty, even a hundredfold.' And he said, 'Listen, anyone who has ears to hear.'

Jesus spoke to his followers in terms of the world they lived in: that mainly agricultural world of villages with their farmers, local officials, and peasant households, and of the countryside with its sheep, vineyards, fishing and crops.

He took his pictures from the world they shared, and, since the prophets had done the same, many of the pictures he used in his parables would have reminded his listeners of the great events that God had promised.

So it's hardly surprising when Jesus describes someone sowing in the fields. Going along the country roads, he must often have pointed to the fields and encouraged those around him to consider what that familiar but always marvellous process of sowing and reaping might help them to understand about him. And when he did so, the echoes of those promised events would have rung in their minds.

Isaiah was one prophet[1] who had compared the fruitfulness of the word of God with the annual marvel in the fields. Don't we see every year, he had said, the rain and snow watering the earth, 'making it yield and giving growth to provide seed for the sower and bread for the eating'. Well, you can be just as sure, he had said, that God's word will succeed in what it was sent to do (Isaiah 55:10–11).

It wasn't just general truths about God, however important, that would have come to the minds of Jesus' audience as they looked at the land they worked at. There were the promised events of the future:

> Once more there will be poured on us
> the spirit from above;
> then shall the wilderness be fertile land
> and fertile land become forest

> In the wilderness justice will come to live and integrity in the fertile land;
> integrity will bring peace,
> justice give lasting security.

> My People will live in a peaceful home,
> in safe houses,
> in quiet dwellings.
> Happy will you be, sowing by every stream,
> letting ox and donkey roam free.
> (Isaiah 32: 15–20)

What form would this promised happiness take? Hosea had been quite specific. What would be sowed would be *a people*, God's people, who would once more respond to the God who loved them and so become lovable again:

> I will sow her, God said, in the country,
> I will love Unloved;
> I will say to No-People-of-Mine, 'You are my People',
> and she will answer, 'You are my God.'
> (Hosea 2: 23–4)

Jesus' story ends with a picture of fruitfulness and would have reminded his listeners of God's promises that his word would be effective and that he would restore his people to his love and joy, but it also emphasizes what all his listeners would have known very well from their experience of the countryside: that although Palestine had a good soil, sowing had its hazards. You often had rock that in places was covered only by the thinnest layer of soil, and you had the tough-rooted thorns and the thistles, that were equally disastrous for the seed.² It shouldn't have been difficult for the people around Jesus to see what this story was trying to say to them. In the great sowing of God's word, just as in the sowing you can see any day in the fields, some seed doesn't sprout at all: could those who were totally opposing Jesus not see the tragedy of missing the greatest opportunity of all?

Some seed quickly withered. People came to Jesus for many reasons, some out of curiosity or for free food. Their loyalty to him was perhaps sincere, but shallow. Could this story help them appreciate that they stood the risk of losing so much?

Then those who were really trying to follow him could be helped by the story to understand several things more clearly about their own situation. Like the *Tares* and the *Dragnet* stories, it could help them appreciate that being a follower of Jesus didn't guarantee success; you still had to resist your tendencies to evil and shallowness. You had to be determined to be wheat, not weed. It could help to restore your confidence in Jesus, in spite of the many setbacks and failures, by reminding you that the sowing of God, like the sowing of the farmer, was likely to have failures.

But though the story starts with three kinds of failure, it ends with three measures of success. That was surely its chief message to Jesus' followers. We all know about the patches of thin soil, the thistles and the thorns, Jesus was telling them. But for the seed that escapes these hazards, don't we get individual grains yielding thirty, sixty or even a hundredfold? Think what kind of yield there will be in *my* sowing!

REFLECTION

1. In developed countries, the equivalent to sowing might be investment in some company. We hope that our investment will be 'fruitful'. But economic forces, we know, are

often unpredictable, even in what seems to be the safest of companies.

But sowing is different. Farming has its hazards and failures, of course. But the basic movement of nature is from seed to harvest.[3] This was the bedrock on which the lives of all of Jesus' listeners were built, immemorially valid and basically dependable.

God's work for his people's 'fruitfulness' was seen by the Jews as equally central in life, equally 'natural' and dependable. God 'plants' his people like a vine; he clears a space where it can grow; and, if his people choose to co-operate with him, indeed there is growth! (Psalm 80: 8–11).

So by painting a simple and realistic picture of the ordinary process of sowing of his country, Jesus not only reminds us of God's promises expressed through the image of sowing, but also enables us to feel the sheer 'naturalness' and dependability of his work with us. From seed there *is* a fine yield, if the growth goes right. That is the rhythm of nature. It's no less the rhythm of the Kingdom.

2. This parable isn't about a harvest in a general sense, but about the yield or lack of it in individual seeds. It tries to help us see the great and wonderful process in which we are being asked to join. But this process is *for* my full development as a person. That is the only reason it was begun. Unless I am wholly involved, with all my powers of heart and mind, of enjoyment and commitment, it cannot achieve its purpose for me.

NOTES

1. The power of this parable comes partly from the fact that it describes realistically a natural process.[4] 'Here are things that you can be confident will happen in nature', it says. 'Can't you be equally sure that similar failures and successes are to be expected in the proclamation of the Kingdom, and therefore shouldn't you take practical steps and adjust your attitudes accordingly?' In order to respond to this we need to avoid the mistake (made by some commentators) of seeing the 'thirty-fold, sixty-fold and a hundred-fold' as fantastic successes. In fact such yields from grains

were good, but far from the best recorded, and it is possible that thirty-fold was quite normal in Palestine in Jesus' time.

II. This particular parable isn't directly about the sower: he comes in only to put the process into operation. Nor is it directly about a harvest, since it is concerned with the fruitfulness, or lack of it, of *individual* seeds.[5]

III. The Gospels show Jesus giving his own interpretation of this parable, as he did in several others. Many of the best writers on the parables hold that 'the interpretation of the parable cannot possibly come from Jesus, as is proved by considerations of language and content.'[6] These considerations of language and content have now been thoroughly examined and have been found to be defective.[7] The interpretation doesn't change or add to the meaning of the parable, but simply draws it out – as one might expect of an interpretation! Matthew's version of the interpretation may preserve a valuable clue as to the meaning of 'the word' which is 'sown', when he calls it 'the word *of the Kingdom*'.

'Sowing' the word of the Kingdom seems to mean *its proclamation*.[8] It seems unnecessary to understand 'proclamation' here as exclusively, or even mainly concerned with *verbal* proclamation or teaching. We know that Jesus helped people realize what the Kingdom is more through his own personality and his actions than just through words.

CHAPTER 4 What did Jesus say about his Teaching in Parables?

From Mark 4: 1–34 (for the Parable of the Sower and its interpretation, see pages 75–9)

1–9 THE PARABLE OF THE SOWER

10–18 When he was alone, the Twelve, together with the others closely associated with him, questioned him about the parables. He told them, 'The hidden reality of the Kingdom of God is given to you, but to those outside, all things are imparted in riddles, so that the Scripture is verified which says that "they may look and look, but see nothing; unless they may turn to God and be forgiven." '

He said to them, 'Do you not understand this parable? Then how will you understand any of the parables?'

14–20 THE INTERPRETATION OF THE PARABLE OF THE SOWER

21–25 He also said to them, 'Would you bring in a lamp to put it under a tub or under the bed? Surely you would put it on the lamp-stand? For there is nothing hidden but it must be disclosed, nothing kept secret except to be brought to light. If anyone has ears to hear, let him listen to this.'

He also said to them, 'Take notice of what you are hearing. The measure you give is the measure you will receive, with something more besides. For the man who has will be given more, and the man who has not will forfeit even what he has.'

26–29 THE PARABLE OF THE SEED GROWING BY ITSELF

30–32 THE PARABLE OF THE MUSTARD SEED

33–34 Using many parables like these, he spoke the word to them so far as they were capable of understanding it. He would not speak to them except in parables, but he explained everything to his disciples when they were alone.

Mark evidently composed a large part of his fourth chapter (1–34) to offer us a lesson about how we can hear Jesus' message spoken in parables.[1] We can't be sure that the sayings of Jesus he gives in this section were originally connected, so for trustworthy results we shall refrain from assuming that they were.

The parable of the *Sower* and its interpretation showed us Jesus reassuring his listeners that his proclamation of the Kingdom, in action and word, could be relied upon to bear fruit in anyone who was truly receptive of it. After the parable of the *Sower*, we find Jesus being 'questioned about the parables'. Now, to Jesus' contemporaries, as we have seen, a parable was a dark perplexing saying or riddle (or action) that is meant to stimulate hard thinking.[2] The parable of the *Sower* was a whole collection of such riddles or parables. So it's quite possible that Jesus' friends were really asking him about the meaning of that particular parable.[3]

WHAT DID JESUS SAY ABOUT HIS TEACHING?

One way or another,[4] they were asking him how his teaching came to people.

There's no reason to suppose that these questioners had gained nothing from Jesus' parables. As the people 'closely associated with him',[5] and in contrast to 'those outside', they must already have partly understood them and been moved by them to come close to him. Nor were they necessarily perplexed that Jesus used parables in his teaching. The rabbis themselves did the same. And learning, in any age, naturally requires the learners to be stimulated to think for themselves.[6] But a parable, or riddle, was something that you could explore more deeply; and they wanted Jesus to help them do that.

In his reply to their question, Jesus underlines the reason why his parables always invite us to greater depths. Those who respond to his parables (as by asking questions to deepen their understanding of their meaning) have the greatest favour of all given them, a full measure of 'the hidden reality of the Kingdom of God'.[7] We have the reality of God's powerful presence in us: not just, or even chiefly, in our minds, but in the way we love and feel and see things. But it is up to us whether it flickers coldly in our lives or boldly and warmly. The parables provide much of the challenge. They invite us to use our mind, our imagination and our experience of life to perceive more clearly that presence of God within us and to commit ourselves in wonder and thankfulness to what we have perceived.

But what about those who haven't been given that fuller measure of the hidden reality of the Kingdom? Before turning to Jesus' apparently harsh answer to this, we may like to remember that in a saying of his recounted later in the chapter he also throws light on this problem, so that although they were possibly said at different times, we should consider the two comments together. There he says: 'Take notice of what you are hearing; the measure you give is the measure you will receive, with something more besides. For the man who has will be given more, and the man who has not will forfeit even what he has.'

The crux, Jesus says here, is the decision about *the generosity of our response*. And this seems to suggest that those

WHAT DID JESUS SAY ABOUT HIS TEACHING? 83

who fail to get much beyond the dark riddle or parable to the good news it tries to help us wrestle with and grasp, owe their failure to their own refusal to respond to Jesus' invitation. The phrase by which Jesus describes them, 'those outside', was the one the rabbis used for those Gentiles or unbelieving Jews who stood outside the Jewish community.[8] They could not be led into the fuller measure of the truth. In fact, in their own interest, the rabbis shielded them from an expression of it, since they would find it too difficult to implement or understand.[9]

Jesus was using the same words the rabbis used to describe people who would not or could not be moved by his teaching and come into his 'community'. His parables, therefore, were not intended to exclude people, but to invite and to help those who could to grapple for themselves with what he was doing and saying, and to shield those who at present couldn't manage that from more of the truth than they could bear.

Not only the evidence just given but also the impression we get of Jesus from his parables and elsewhere inclines us to accept that conclusion. But isn't it refuted by Jesus' saying:

> But to those who are outside, all things are imparted in riddles;
> so that they may look and look, but see nothing;
> they may hear and hear, but understand nothing;
> unless they may turn to God and be forgiven.

Now Jesus is quoting from a passage here from Isaiah that reads like a condemnation to exclusion from the light,[10] but which in Jesus' time seems to have been interpreted as a promise of forgiveness on repentance. He seems deliberately to have quoted it, not from the Hebrew Bible, but from the version used in the synagogue which was interpreted in that way. The key to the change came in understanding the first word of the last line as 'unless', instead of a possible 'so that they won't'.[11] What confirms the view that the quotation from Isaiah was not being used to say that God had condemned a certain group of people to ignorance and condemnation is that later in this Gospel (8:17,21) Jesus rebukes *his disciples* in words taken from the same passage of Isaiah.

'You are being blind to what you see me doing', he is saying to them in effect. 'I beg you really to turn your minds and hearts to what I am offering you.'

If we move further through Mark's chapter, we come to more evidence on Jesus' purpose in teaching through parables:

> Nothing is hidden (i.e. expressed in 'riddles')
> except in order that it may be revealed;
> Nothing is concealed,
> except in order that it may come to light.[12]

The intention is to reveal, for in a typically homely expression, Jesus compares the Kingdom to a lamp, and a lamp is obviously there for giving light, not for being hidden. But he goes on to point out, as we have seen, that whether this 'hidden' thing illumines you or not depends on the quality of your responsiveness: 'the measure you give is the measure you receive.'

So Jesus gave 'the word' to his audiences 'in the measure that they were able to receive it' (v. 33). And because it was the best way to help them to see and respond to him, 'he would not speak to them except in parables' (v. 34). To those who did respond enough to want to deepen their comprehension and commitment, he was glad to give help by further explanation. No doubt he did this 'privately' because those not so disposed would misunderstand what he said. But in the tense political situation of the time, when misunderstandings about plans to resist the authorities were liable to lead very swiftly to execution, Jesus would have had other motives for privacy as well.

NOTE

Was there some unity originally in this collection of pieces in Mark? A practice of the rabbis was to use a parable to answer or challenge the argument of an outsider and then, when again alone with his disciples, when asked for a better answer than could be understood by outsiders, to give a fuller interpretation. It has been plausibly argued that Jesus may have given the parable of the *Sower* in response to a question from an outsider about the meaning of

WHAT DID JESUS SAY ABOUT HIS TEACHING?

Isaiah 6: 9–10.[13] Then afterwards his disciples asked him for a fuller explanation (v. 10). Jesus is astonished that they, who had had first-hand experience of the breaking-in of the Kingdom, need further explanation of a parable that expresses such a fundamental point (vv. 11–13), but then goes on to give the explanation nevertheless.[14] Others would say that vv. 11–12 are themselves the interpretation of the parable and would dispute that 14–20 could have been spoken by Jesus (cf. page 79). Other suggestions for finding an original unity have also been made.[15] Certainty, or even a great degree of probability, seems at present impossible to achieve.

ENDNOTES

Abbreviations used in these endnotes

Bible versions:
JB	*Jerusalem Bible*
NEB	*New English Bible*
RSV	*Revised Standard Version*

Books:
K. Bailey, *Poet*	K. E. Bailey, *Poet and Peasant*. Grand Rapids 1976
J. Derrett, *Law*	J. D. M. Derrett, *Law in the New Testament*. London 1970
J. Jeremias, *Parables*	J. Jeremias, *The Parables of Jesus*. London 1963
E. Linnemann, *Parables*	E. Linnemann, *Parables of Jesus*. London 1966
I. Howard Marshall, *Luke*	I. Howard Marshall, *The Gospel of Luke*. Exeter 1978
TDNT	G. Kittel and G. Friedrich, ed., *Theological Dictionary of the New Testament*. Grand Rapids 1964–76

Periodicals:
JBL	*Journal of Biblical Literature*
JTS	*Journal of Theological Studies* (new series)
NT	*Novum Testamentum*
NTS	*New Testament Studies*

ZNW *Zeitschrift für die Neuetestamentliche Wissenschaft*

Chapter 1 Speaking in Parables (pp. 1–7)

[1] C.E.B. Cranfield, 'St Mark: 4: 1–34', *Scottish Journal of Theology* 4 (1951), p. 407.
[2] Needless to say, any schematization of Jesus' parables can at best be approximate. The one I have adopted for this book and for *More Parables for Now* is that given by J. Dupont in *Pourquoi des paraboles* (Paris 1977), pp. 26–40.

The Prodigal Son (pp. 11–20)

[1] *The text* It has been argued quite recently that the parable was composed by Luke (L. Schottroff, 'Das Gleichnis vom verlorenen Sohn', *Zeitschrift für Theologie und Kirche* (1971), pp. 27–52), and it has also been argued that only the first half of the parable came from Jesus, the rest from Luke or another writer (J. Sanders, 'Tradition and Redaction in Luke 15: 11–32', *NTS*, 15 (1969), pp. 433–8). But it is generally accepted that the overwhelming probability is that the parable was composed by Jesus. It presupposes a close knowledge of Jewish law and social custom (cf. K. Bailey, *Poet*, pp. 161–203; J. Derrett, pp. 104–12), the Old Testament allusions are from the Hebrew, not the Greek text (O. Hofius, 'Alttestamentliche Motive im Gleichnis vom verlorenen Sohn', *NTS*, 24 (1978), pp. 246–8), much of the language is not Lucan (in both halves of the parable) and the attitude to the Pharisees (very roughly suggested by the elder brother) and the theology are not Lucan, but fit well with what we know of Jesus' life and teaching (C.E. Carlston, 'Reminiscence and Redaction in Luke 15: 11–32', *JBL*, 94 (1975), pp. 368–90; and I. Broer, 'Der Verschwender und die Theologie des Lukas', *NTS*, 20 (1974), p. 462). These considerations, and the structure of the story, seem to make it virtually certain that the parable was originally basically the unit we now have.
[2] On the 'younger brother' mythology in Jewish tradition cf. J. D. Derrett, *Law*, pp. 116–19; and Bernard B. Scott, 'The Prodigal Son: a structuralist interpretation', *Semeia*, 9 (1977), pp. 62–3.
[3] For the details of the social background of this story, see especially K. Bailey, *Poet*, pp. 161–203.
[4] Cf. especially Jeremiah 31: 18–20.
[5] The clear and strong echoes of this Esau-Jacob incident (especially in Genesis 33: 4) in use of language, in the way it fits into their respective stories, and in content has been shown recently by O. Hofius, pp. 246–8.
[6] The meaning of the word (cf. I. Howard Marshall, *Luke*, p. 612).

[7] The open-ended character of this parable has been stressed by several recent critics: particularly by Bernard B. Scott, art. cit., pp. 45–74; and F. Schnider, 'Das Gleichnis vom verlorenen Schaf und seine Redaktoren', *Kairos* (1977), p. 148. K. Bailey shows how the structure of the second half of the parable underlines this open-endedness: the structure sets up an expectation of reconciliation and shared celebration, but leaves the stanza that should satisfy the expectation missing, *Poet*, p. 191.
[8] I. Howard Marshall, *Luke*, p. 607.
[9] Cf. I. Howard Marshall, ibid., p. 609; and K. Bailey, *Poet*, pp. 173–6.
[10] Cf. I. Howard Marshall, ibid., pp. 610–11.

The Lost Sheep (pp. 21–28)

[1] J. D. Derrett, 'Fresh Light on the Lost Sheep and the Lost Coin', *NTS* 26 (1979), pp. 38–40.
[2] K. Bailey, *Poet*, p. 149.
[3] C. Stuhlmueller, 'The Gospel according to Luke', in *Jerome Bible Commentary* (London 1968), p. 148; and cf. K. Bailey, ibid., p. 148.
[4] Cf. J. Jeremias, *Parables*, p. 134.
[5] Cf. K. Bailey, *Poet*, p. 149.
[6] Cf. F. Schnider, *Die verlorenen Söhne* (Göttingen 1977), pp. 28–42, 85–7. On the theological background, cf. H. Geist, 'Jesus vor Israel – der Ruf zur Sammlung', in K. Muller, ed., *Die Aktion Jesu und die Re-Aktion der Kirche* (Wurzburg 1972), pp. 31–63; and G. Lohfink, *Die Sammlung Israels: eine Untersuchung zur lukanischen Ekklesiologie* (Munich 1975).
[7] J. Jeremias, *Parables*, p. 133; cf. J. Derrett, art. cit., p. 59. E. Linnemann denies this: 'The similitude says nothing of this; its effectiveness would be lost if this feature were introduced, and the contrast 1: 99 would lose its effectiveness' (*Parables*, p. 65). Linnemann was right to underline the importance of the contrast. But the contrast is one of *attention to* the one more than to the ninety-nine at the two moments described, not *to sacrificing the safety of* ninety-nine for the sake of the one.
[8] Opinions about the authenticity of many parts of the parable differ considerably. Two scholars who have recently made detailed analyses of the parable have concluded that except for the phrase 'who have no need of repentance', Luke gives us the parable as he found it (F. Schnider, op. cit., pp. 75–7 and 85, and J. Jeremias, 'Tradition und Redaktion in Lukas 15', *ZNW*, 62 (1971), pp. 184–5, and *Die Sprache des Lukasevangeliums* (Göttingen 1980), p. 248), though this does not of course say that what he found was Jesus' original version.

In fact it seems probable that, except for one verb of Luke ('loses' in v. 4), Matthew gives the earlier version *where the two texts run parallel* (cf. J. Dupont, 'La parabole de la brebis perdue', *Gregorianum*, 49 (1968), pp. 273–9, and in 'Les implications christologiques de la parabole de la brebis perdue', in J. Dupont, ed., *Jesus aux origines de la Christologie* (Louvain 1975), pp. 334–5 and note 9 – though F. Schnider would largely disagree, op. cit., pp. 75–6. It is also generally agreed that Matthew's application of the parable, and at least 'who have no need of repentance' in Luke, are not original. This leaves us with two further questions about the text: were Luke's verses 5 and 6 (which are without parallel in Matthew) and was most of his verse 7 original or not?

On verses 5 and 6 Linnemann states categorically that they 'cannot be original', since it would be wrong to think that the shepherd would have brought 'the sheep from the wilderness of the hill-country into the inhabited area, instead of bringing it back as quickly as possible to the flock that he had left on its own' (*Parables*, p. 68). But her argument here seems to be refuted by the evidence we have from J. Derrett and K. Bailey, given in the commentary, about the habits of Palestinian shepherds. These verses seem therefore to be basically original, though with Lucan linguistic embellishments (cf. J. Dupont, 'La parabole de la brebis', art. cit., pp. 277–8).

So far as the first two thirds of v. 7 are concerned, the matter is disputed. J. Dupont holds that Luke changed Matthew (*'Les implications christologiques'*, art. cit., p. 335 and notes 12 and 13), while J. Jeremias holds that Luke inherited the piece (*Die Sprache des Lukasevangeliums*, op. cit., pp. 246–7). Its message is already implicit in the parable, in our interpretation of it. And if the structure of the parable advanced by K. Bailey is correct (*Poet*, p. 144 and cf. Linnemann, *Parable*, p. 70 note h), it is most probable that they were original, except for the explicit mention of repentance, which was a Lucan preoccupation and which damages the structure. My slightly amended version of Bailey's reconstruction adjusts (I hope) to all these factors.

The Lost Coin (pp. 29–31)

[1] For this text cf K. Bailey, *Poet*, p. 156. I have adapted his text so as to render it into prose.

[2] For the details of the picture conveyed by the story, cf. J. Jeremias, *Parables*, pp. 134–5; J. Derrett, 'Fresh Light on the Lost Sheep and the Lost Coin', *NTS*, 26 (1979), pp. 40–2, 45; K. Bailey, *Poet*, pp. 156–8.

[3] Cf. J. Derrett, ibid., p. 51.

[4] J. Jeremias believes that because the number comes *before* the noun in the *Sheep* parable and *after* it in the *Coin* parable, we must conclude that they didn't originally belong together (*Die Sprache des Lukasevangeliums* (Göttingen 1980), p. 245). He earlier showed that apart from slight stylistic retouching, Luke has reproduced it as he found it ('Tradition und Redaktion in Lukas 15', *ZNW*, 62 (1971), pp. 184–5). The Aramaic puns (on *zuzim* and on 'one'/'joy'), the details of Palestinian life presupposed, and the parable's relevance to Jesus' situation are strong arguments for its authenticity.

The Workers in the Vineyard (pp. 32–42)

[1] For 'are your hearts filled with rancour', cf. W. Haubeck, 'Zum Verständnis der Parabel von den Arbeitern in Weinberg', in W. Haubeck, ed., *Wort in der Zeit* (Leiden 1980), p. 104. For the other adjustments to the JB version, cf. J. Jeremias, *Parables*, pp. 137–8.

[2] J. Jeremias, *Jerusalem in the Time of Jesus* (London 1967), p. 45; and G. Dalman, *Arbeit und Sitte in Palästina*, volume 4 (Gütersloh 1935), p. 298.

[3] For details see J. Derrett, 'Workers in the Vineyard: a Parable of Jesus', *Journal of Jewish Studies*, 25 (1974), pp. 64–91.

[4] Even if the original parable didn't start with the words 'The Kingdom of God is like', which may well have been the case.

[5] Cf. Jeremiah 31: 31–4.

[6] So Derrett, art. cit., pp. 67–8, arguing against the frequent contention that a denarius was the normal daily wage for an unskilled labourer.

[7] Derrett, art cit., p. 72.

[8] The word translated 'standing idle' (v. 3) implies readiness for activity. Cf. Derrett, art. cit., p. 69 note 14.

[9] Derrett, art. cit., p. 73.

[10] F. C. Glover, 'Workers for the Vineyard', *Expository Times* 86 (1974–5), pp. 310–1); and A. Feuillet, 'Les ouvriers envoyés à la vigne', *Revue Thomiste* 79 (1979), p. 13, would say that the reason was their disinterestedness and total trust in the landowner. But from the merely *story* point of view, other more commonplace explanations would have occurred to the audience. From the point of view of the parable's *message*, the stress in the written story seems to be pivotally on the landowner's reiterated acts of goodness. But in the story in the context in which Jesus spoke it, perhaps the disinterestedness and trust of the tax-collectors in Jesus were so conspicuous that they were quite clearly being alluded to; cf. Derrett, art cit., pp. 73–4.

[11] Derrett, art cit., p. 73 note 37, and pp. 78–9.

[12] In several passages in the Old Testament about God the word *hesed* is simply a complement or clarifying extension of 'good' (*tob*), and in later texts 'good' could replace *hesed*. Cf. H. J. Stoebe, 'tōb', in E. Jenni, ed., *Theologische Handwörterbuch zum Alten Testament* (Munich and Zurich 1975), volume 1 column 662.

[13] Cf. Feuillet, art. cit., p. 21.

[14] Cf. W. Haubeck, art. cit., p. 104, note 33.

[15] F. C. Glover, art. cit., p. 310.

[16] 'It is clear that it is directed against the materialisation of the concept of the alliance, so frequent in the Jewish world' (Feuillet, art. cit., p. 19).

[17] Feuillet would bring 19:30 into evidence in his claim that an exhortation to disinterestedness is a major purpose of the parable. 'Those who will be too preoccupied with their reward run the risk of passing from the first place to the last, while those who give themselves to Christ forgetting themselves like the eleventh-hour workers will be taken up to the first place in as much as they will have the preference of the Lord' (art. cit., p. 15). But the story doesn't say that the first-comers went to the last

place – all had *equal* pay, and the order of payment wasn't material. Also it isn't at all clear that the eleventh-hour workers 'forgot themselves' (how could they forget their families' need of food?). Feuillet admits that v. 15a is fully intelligible only at the theological level (p. 21). If the eleventh-hour workers represent the tax-collectors *as people*, then it is untrue to say that Jesus wished to favour them more than others. Feuillet's theory will work only if they represent chiefly the tax-collectors' *attitudes to Jesus*.

[18] J. Dupont, 'La Parabole des Ouvriers de la Vigne', *Nouvelle Revue Théologique*, 79 (1957), p. 795.

[19] Ibid., p. 788.

[20] J. Jeremias, *Parables*, pp. 36 and 137.

[21] J. Dupont, art. cit., pp. 789–92.

The Great Supper (pp. 43–49)

[1] E. Linnemann, *Parables*, p. 88.

[2] J. Derrett, *Law*, p. 138.

[3] The interpretation of this parable has quite largely hinged on the interpreters' understanding of the three excuses. In the 1960s, the most influential interpretations were Eta Linnemann's (*Parables*, pp. 88–96) and Joachim Jeremias' (*Parables*, particularly pp. 176–80). The former held that the invited guests intended to come after they had completed their business, since according to the custom of Jerusalem, guests could appear up to the end of the first course. The parable proclaims that 'in fact. . . the kingdom of God is already arriving. . . . With tax-collectors and sinners he (Jesus) holds the proleptic celebration of the feast that all Israel is expecting to enjoy in the kingdom of God' (p. 91). The latter held that the excuses were snubs to a tax-gatherer who had become wealthy (p. 179). For the former the parable is saying: *Now* is the acceptable time; the banquet is already begun. The latter begins with a similar understanding and then develops it: not only is the parable challenging the listener to urgent action ('It may be too late'), but also the parable 'is not fully understood until attention is paid to the note of joy which rings through the summons: "everything is ready" ' (p. 180).

There are major difficulties against both these interpretations (e.g. Linnemann has rather arbitrarily to eliminate verse 20 and give a very strained interpretation of 'all alike started to make excuses' whose dominant meaning seems to be 'decline, refuse, reject, avoid', cf. Paul H. Ballard, 'Reasons for Refusing the Great Supper', *Journal of Theological Studies*, 23 (1972), pp. 342–3). Since about 1970, there has been a growing recognition of the importance of the allusion to two passages in Deuteronomy. (Cf. particularly J. Derrett, *Law*, pp. 136–42 and Humphrey Palmer, 'Just Married, Cannot Come', *NT*, (1976), pp. 241–57). We have to remember that allusion to well-known biblical texts was, in Jesus' time, a common way of teaching.

[4] J. D. M. Derrett, *Law*, p. 141. There is a problem here, since the host says to the servant 'I tell you', and the 'you' in the Greek is plural. But

the awareness of Christians using it that it applied to many could easily account for the change.

[5] The Greek text makes it especially clear that *anger* is the cause of all the host's action after he has heard from the servant of the rejection and the excuses: 'then being very angry, the householder said to his servant: 'Go out . . . go out . . . for I tell you . . . ' (vv. 21b–24).

[6] This may well be original (in spite of much earlier scepticism); cf. I. Howard Marshall, p. 587.

[7] There is no doubt that the parable lays great stress on the 'invited' and 'not invited' theme. It starts with a man who 'invited many' to a feast (in Hebrew the word 'many' may well have meant 'his chosen friends') and who sent his servant to tell 'the invited' to come to the feast, and its climax is that not one of 'the invited' will taste of it. In Hebrew and Greek the words for 'invited' and 'called' are the same.

[8] Isaiah 43: 1 and 42: 6–7.

[9] Cf. J. A. Sanders, 'The Ethic of Election in Luke's Great Banquet Parable', in J. L. Crenshaw and John T. Willis, ed., *Essays in Old Testament Ethics* (New York 1974), pp. 245–71, from whom the quotations in this paragraph are taken (pages 262–3). Until this discovery was made, it was cogently argued that the reference to the 'maimed, blind and lame' wasn't in the original story, largely because of its being parallel with 14: 13 (e.g. by F. Hahn, 'Das Gleichnis von der Einladung zum Festmahl', *Verborum Veritas* (Wuppertal 1970), p. 58).

[10] The Greek seems to mean 'all of them unanimously' (I. Howard Marshall, *Luke*, p. 588).

[11] Cf. Isaiah 41:17; 54: 11–17; 58: 7–9; 61:1.

[12] If we lay this story alongside the conversation about the taking the first place of honour at a wedding feast, it is still clearer that Jesus wanted to put into question the currently accepted views about who would be at the feast with the Messiah and concern with man-measured position. Sanders (op. cit., p. 263) has made it evident that *both* passages allude to the kind of élitism that was being propounded at the time at Qumran.

Two Sons (pp. 50–55)

[1] The manuscripts differ as to which son said 'yes' and which said 'no'. The New English Bible favours the version of the first one saying 'yes'. I have here adopted this text because this version preserves the elder son/younger son theme, which may well have been present in the original parable (cf. J. Derrett, 'The Parable of the Two Sons', *Studia Theologica*, 25 (1971), pp. 111 and 116). I have, however, changed the last words of the text from 'ahead of you' to 'rather than you', since it is now generally accepted that this is the meaning: cf. J. Jeremias, *Parables*, p. 125 n. 48, and J. Dupont, 'Les deux fils dissemblables', *Assemblées du Seigneur* 57 (2nd series 1971), p. 25 note 10, though H. Mekel in 'Das Gleichnis von der "ungleichen Söhnen" ', *NTS*, 20 (1973–4), p. 257 note 343, believes that 'the postulated aramaic original is yet to be proved'.

ENDNOTES

[2] After writing this commentary I found that Jacques Dupont saw this parable in the same light: 'Religious practices lose their value if they evoke in a person a self-confidence that blinds him to the call God makes to him through the ministry of Jesus' (op. cit., p. 25).

[3] For details cf. H. Merkel, pp. 255-8.

[4] As he did, for example, in the parable of the Great Supper, where in the original parable the people invited from the streets represented despised Jews, while in Matthew they represent the Gentiles.

[5] Or redrafted it – it may in some form have been added to the original parable before Matthew. On this, and on the typically Matthean expressions in v. 32, cf. Merkel, art. cit.; A. Ogawa, 'Paraboles de l'Israël Véritable? Reconsidération critique de Mt 21: 28–22: 14', *NT*, 21 (1979), pp. 122-4; and R. Hummel, *Die Auseinandersetzung zwischen Kirche und Judentum im Matthäusevangelium* (Munich 1963), p. 23.

[6] J. Derrett translates: 'to show you the right way to live' in art. cit., p. 115, as does Dupont, art. cit., p. 30.

[7] Noted by R. Hummel, op. cit., p. 23.

[8] W. Trilling, 'Die Taufertradition bei Matthäus', *Biblische Zeitschrift*, 3 (1959), p. 274.

[9] David E. Garland, 'The Intention of Matthew 23', *Supplements to Novum Testamentum*, 52 (1979) (Leiden), p. 45. As Walter Wink wrote, 'Matthew concentrates on the Pharisees as the real opponents of Jesus, and at every opportunity makes them the villains of the piece' (*John the Baptist in the Gospel Tradition* (Cambridge 1968), p. 34).

The Mustard Seed and the Leaven (pp. 58–62)

[1] For this text cf. H. K. McArthur, 'The Parables of the Mustard Seed', *Catholic Biblical Quarterly*, 33 (1971), p. 200.

[2] As a metaphor, leaven normally had, for a Jew, a strongly negative association. But sometimes it could be used positively, as of the leavening influence of the Torah. Evocative ambivalence of this kind was part of Jesus' art as a religious story-teller.

[3] John Dominic Crossan, *In Parables* (New York 1973), p. 51.

[4] Not in the Gospel of Thomas. But this tends to eliminate or diminish Old Testament allusion.

[5] Cf. Robert W. Funk, 'Beyond Criticism in Quest of Literacy', *Interpretation*, 25 (1971), pp. 159-62.

[6] 'Hidden' tends to suggest in the Gospels the profound presence of God that must be searched for if it is to be found and can be discovered only by those who are willing to respond to him; cf. Robert W. Funk, art. cit., pp. 158-9.

[7] I am assuming that these two parables are to be seen as a pair. J. Dupont has pointed to the weakness of the arguments for their being separate in the earliest version and has given reasons why they should probably be seen as a pair (in 'Le couple parabolique du sénevé et du levain', in G.

Strecker, ed., *Jesus Christ in Historie und Theologie* (Tübingen 1975), pp. 331–45).

[8] Several scholars consider it unlikely that Jesus alluded to this passage of Ezekiel when he told the story. I must explain why I differ from them: (1) For the reasons given by J. Dupont (art. cit., pp. 331–45) it seems very likely that the *Leaven* and *Mustard Seed* parables were very early a pair. (2) It is acknowledged that before Q (i.e. in the 40s or 50s), the *Mustard Seed* parable had this allusion (cf. H. K. McArthur, art. cit., p. 206). But it is claimed that this allusion was added to Jesus' original parable as the Church reflected more fully on his role as Messiah-Saviour, and that Jesus himself couldn't have made the allusion himself because to start a story culminating in this great allusion to the cedar with a mere mustard seed would be burlesque. But once we accept that the parables are a pair and recognize that the spirit of the *Leaven* parable is one of comic exaggeration, the main difficulty against accepting the allusion as Jesus' vanishes. (3) The other important difficulty has already found an answer by J. Dupont art. cit., p. 341 note 35: a bush *can* be referred to as a tree: Josephus calls a hyssop a tree (*Jewish Antiquities*, VIII. 44).

The Seed Growing Secretly (pp. 63–68)

[1] It is very possible that the introduction 'The Kingdom of God is like' is not original, since these introductory formulas appear and disappear in the course of transmission too often for one to be sure that they were in every case in the original version; but the Joel allusion shows that the parable is nevertheless about the Kingdom. Some recent authors have maintained that verses 28 and 29 are not from the original. But their arguments seem to me to have been refuted by J. Dupont, in 'Encore la parabole de la Semence qui pousse toute seule', in E. Earle Ellis and Erich Grässer ed., *Jesus und Paulus* (Göttingen 1975), pp. 96–108. It has been suggested that we have *two* parables here: an earlier one encouraging patient confidence about the apparently delayed Final Coming (verses 26, part of 27 and 29) and a later one hinging on *automate*, teaching that the coming of the Kingdom does not *depend* on our actions and their apparent success or failure (27, 28a): H.-W. Kuhn, *Ältere Sammlungen im Markusevangelium* (Göttingen 1971), pp. 104–112. Kuhn's interpretation of *automate*, which he agrees is crucial for the interpretation of 27f, seems to conflict with the evidence (cf. R. Stuhlmann, 'Beobachtungen und Überlegungen zu Markus IV. 26–29', *NTS*, 19 (1973), pp. 153–62). His thesis mainly arises from the view that 'a parable, in contrast to an allegory, can demonstrate only *one* point' (art. cit., p. 106), helped by his belief that the quotation from Joel 4: 13 presupposes the Hebrew text (p. 111), disputed by Dupont (art. cit., pp. 102–3). But there seems to be no reason why a parable should not turn on an antithetic contrast, particularly if the two situations contrasted have a considerable continuity between them. This continuity is reinforced by the special sense of *automate* discerned by Stuhlmann. The interpretation given here is more fully argued by Dupont,

'La parabole de la semence qui pousse toute seule', *Recherches de Science Religieuse*, 55 (1967), pp. 367–92; idem, 'Encore la parabole. . .', art. cit. (1975), pp. 96–108; and W. G. Kümmel, 'Noch einmal: Das Gleichnis von der selbstwachsenden Saat', *Orientierung an Jesus: Zur Theologie der Synoptiker*, ed. P. Hoffmann, (Freiburg im Breisgau 1973), pp. 220–37.

The Tares and The Dragnet (pp. 69–74)

[1] For the text of the parable of the *Tares*, cf. David R. Catchpole, 'John the Baptist, Jesus and the Parable of the Tares', *Scottish Journal of Theology*, 31 (1978), pp. 557–70. For the text of the parable of the *Dragnet*, it is generally agreed that vv. 49–50 didn't belong to the original parable; cf. ibid., pp. 558–9.
[2] Cf. J. Jeremias, *Parables*, p. 225.
[3] Cf. e.g. Strack-Billerbeck, *Kommentar zum Neuen Testament* (Munich 1961), vol. i, p. 673; and 112, p. 232.
[4] For the details in the last two parables, cf. especially P. Franz Dunkel, 'Die Fischerei am See Genesareth und das N.T.', *Biblica*, 5 (1924), pp. 375–90; and G. Dalman, *Orte und Wege Jesu* (Guterslöh 1919), pp. 132–5; A. E. Ross, 'Nets', in J. Hastings, ed., *Dictionary of Christ and the Gospels* (Edinburgh) 1923f, vol. ii, p. 242.
[5] It is generally accepted that the interpretation of the parable of the *Tares* (i.e. vv. 36–43) is the work of Matthew; cf. e.g. J. Jeremias, *Parables* pp. 81–5). So far as *the parable* is concerned, M. D. Goulder, *Midrash and Lection in Matthew* (London 1974), pp. 367–9, believes that this parable is a Matthean version of the Marcan *Seed Growing Secretly*. Of the nine reasons given for this view, most either lapse or are considerably reduced in force if David R. Catchpole's reconstruction of the original parable, that we have adopted, is accepted. The only two reasons that would remain in full force would be ' (a) the *order* of Mark 4 is *Sower*, Reason of Parables, Interpretation of Sower, Appended Sayings, *Seed Growing Secretly*, *Mustard Seed*. Matthew has the first three and last, with the Appended Sayings elsewhere, and the *Tares* in place of the *Seed Growing Secretly*. (b) There is *no* other considerable unit of Mark omitted in Matthew. In all cases of apparent omission of a paragraph we find a Matthaeanized version somewhere in the Gospel' (pp. 367–8). Against this it could be argued that 'Since Matthew has just stressed the need for bearing fruit, it would not be to his purpose to include the parable of the seed that grows even when no attention is paid to it.' (Eduard Schweizer, *The Good News According to Matthew* (London 1976), p. 302). It would in any case have been typical of Matthew to have introduced an emphasis on judgement (as he also does through inserting the Parable of the *Dragnet* later in *his* 'chapter of parables' and by adding vv. 49–50 to that parable. 'L'application du thème du jugement à l'Eglise constitue précisément un *novum* de la théologie matthéenne à l'égard de ses sources Marc et Q.' (Daniel Marguerat, 'L'Eglise et le monde en Matthieu 13:36–43', *Revue de*

Théologie et de Philosophie 110 (1978), p. 124, note 63 and works there cited).

[6] Matthew normally uses 'Lord' to attribute divine authority and exalted status to Jesus; see Georg Strecker, *Der Weg der Gerechtigkeit* (Göttingen 1962), p. 123; and J. D. Kingsbury, *Matthew: Structure, Christology, Kingdom* (London 1976), p. 124.

[7] Others would say that while *in the parable* Matthew is speaking about the Church, *in the interpretation* he is speaking about the world (especially J. Dupont, 'Le chapitre des Paraboles', in M. Didier, ed., L'Evangile selon Matthieu: Rédaction et Théologie (Gembloux 1972), pp. 228–9. I find the view of Daniel Marguerat more persuasive, partly for the reasons he gives (art. cit.) and partly because it removes the unlikely inconsistency between Matthew's purpose in editing the parable and in composing the interpretation. It is true that Matthew says that 'the field is the world' (v. 38). But it seems wrong to argue (as, recently, Russell Pregeant, *Christology Beyond Dogma: Matthew's Christ in Process Hermeneutic* (Philadelphia 1978), pp. 108–10) from this that Matthew has explicitly in mind here the relationship of the world (i.e. the Church *and* those outside it) to judgement. 'World' in that verse, as D. Marguerat points out (art. cit., p. 116) isn't the place of judgement, but the place where the seed is sown: where the Church exercises her *universal* mission; cf. W. Trilling, *Das Wahre Israel* (Leipzig 1958), pp. 101–3. It is relevant to add that in Matthew's concluding parable of this section (the *Dragnet*), he has explicitly the Church in mind, not the world; cf. J. D. Kingsbury, *The Parables of Jesus in Matthew 13* (London 1969), p. 121; and M. D. Goulder, op cit., p. 374.

The Sower (pp. 75–79)

[1] Strangely, the Old Testament background is often neglected in modern interpretations of this parable. Yet it was clearly indicated long ago by Sir E. Hoskyns and N. Davey, *The Riddle of the New Testament* (London 1931), pp. 163–6 (though they mistakenly, in my view, consider harvest to be a central image of this parable).

[2] Cf. E. Linnemann, *Parables*, p. 115; and G. Dalman, *Orte und Wege Jesu* (Guterslöh 1924), p. 130.

[3] Cf. *TDNT*, vii, p. 541 (G. Quell).

[4] Cf. P. B. Payne, 'The Authenticity of the Parable of the Sower and its Interpretation', in R. T. France, ed., *Gospel Perspectives*, vol.i (Sheffield 1980), pp. 181–6.

[5] Ibid., p. 181. But it isn't adequate to say simply that 'the emphasis is on the responsibility of the hearer' (G. B. Caird, in a review in *JTS*, 29 (1978), p. 534), because the emphasis is also on the assurance of the fruitfulness of God's climactic sowing of his word. The parable both warns and encourages, as Payne notes (ibid., p. 167).

[6] E. Linnemann, *Parables*, p. 185 note 16, referring to J. Jeremias, *Parables*, pp. 77–9. More recently, and just as dismissive, is J. Kirkland, 'The

Earliest Understanding of Jesus's Use of Parables', *NT*, 19 (1977), p. 16, who says that it is almost universally admitted to be a later accretion, except by C. F. Moule, whose arguments are 'hasty and unconvincing'. In 1951 C.E.B. Cranfield gave a systematic study of the data and came to the conclusion that it is 'rather more likely that the explanation goes back to Jesus than that it does not'. ('St Mark 4: 1–34', *Scottish Journal of Theology*, 4 (1951), pp. 405–12). C. F. D. Moule, in a balanced discussion, came to the conclusion that it can 'at least plausibly be attributed to Jesus himself'. ('Mark 4: 1–20 yet once more', in E. E. Ellis, ed., *Neotestamentica et Semitica* (Edinburgh 1969), p. 113). E. Trocmé believes that it was written by Mark ('Why Parables? A study of Mark IV', in *The Bulletin of the John Rylands Library*, 59 (1977), pp. 465–6). M. Boucher believes that 'arguments on either side fall short of conclusiveness' (*The Mysterious Parable* (Washington 1977), p. 53).
[7] By P. B. Payne, op. cit., pp. 169–86.
[8] P. B. Payne, ibid., pp. 179, and 201, note 53.

What Did Jesus say about his Teaching in Parables? (pp. 80–85)

[1] Cf. M. Boucher, *The Mysterious Parable* (Washington 1977), p. 43.
[2] Cf. C. Cranfield, art. cit., p. 407; E. Trocmé, art. cit., p. 461; and (on *action*) G. H. Boobyer, 'The Redaction of Mark 4: 1–34', *NTS*, 8 (1961–2), pp. 63–4.
[3] A view advanced most recently by E. Trocmé (art. cit., pp. 461–2). Jesus here explains in terms of what takes place what he had expressed in parabolic form to the crowd (cf. I. Howard Marshall, *Luke*, p. 323).
[4] The two views aren't mutually exclusive (cf. J. R. Kirkland, 'The Earliest Understanding of Jesus's Use of Parables: Mark IV: 10–12 in Context', *NT*, 19 (1977), p. 5).
[5] For this interpretation of the phrase, cf. J. W. Bowker, art. cit., p. 309.
[6] Cf. E. Linnemann, *Parables*, pp. 18–23; and C. F. D. Moule, 'Mark 4: 1–20 yet once more', in E. E. Ellis, ed., *Neotestamentica et Semitica* (Edinburgh 1969), pp. 96–7.
[7] Cf. K. Haacker, 'Erwägungen zu Mc 4: 11', *NT*, 14 (1972), pp. 219–20. E. Trocmé (art. cit., p. 462) notes that 'we must avoid introducing the idea of *knowledge* acquired from the parables.' It is a question of getting hold of the Kingdom of God. S. Brown emphasizes the knowledge or instruction side of *Mark's* (as opposed to Jesus') understanding of the parable of the Sower (S. Brown, 'The Secret of the Kingdom', *JBL*, 92 (1973), pp. 62–74).
[8] G. Haufe, 'Erwägungen zum Ursprung der sogenannten Parabeltheorie Markus 4: 11–12', *Evangelische Theologie*, 32 (1972), p. 416.
[9] J. W. Bowker, art. cit., p. 304.
[10] As C. F. D. Moule says (art. cit., p. 100): 'It is difficult to believe that, in its original context in Isaiah 6, it was intended as an instruction to the prophet to make sure that his message was unintelligible.'

[11] J. Jeremias, *Parables*, pp. 15–18. J. Kirkland (art. cit., p. 7) discusses alternative, but largely analogous, renderings.

[12] I have given, roughly, J. Kirkland's translation; cf. art. cit., pp. 12–13.

[13] This view has been put forward by, among others, J. Jeremias, *Parables*, p. 15. It has been strongly argued against by D. Wenham, 'The Synoptic Problem Revisited: some new suggestions about the composition of Mark 4: 1–34', *Tyndale Bulletin*, 23 (1972), p. 25, note 59.

[14] J. W. Bowker, art. cit., pp. 310–13.

[15] J. Kirkland, art. cit., pp. 16–21; E. Lemcio, 'External Evidence for the Structure and Function of Mark IV: 1 – 20', *JTS*, NS 29 (1978), pp. 323–38.